MY FIVE SONS

MY FIVE SONS

Rachel Nutter

iUniverse, Inc.
New York Bloomington Shanghai

MY FIVE SONS

Copyright © 2008 by Rachel Nutter

iUniverse books may be ordered through booksellers or by contacting:

iUniverse
1663 Liberty Drive
Bloomington, IN 47403
www.iuniverse.com
1-800-Authors (1-800-288-4677)

Prepare Picture Pages	Marvin Sandlin
Reproduced Pictures	Xiaodan Ke
Photo-Insert Design	Lam Huynh
Cover Design	Xiaodan Ke

First Edition
Copy Shoppe Printers Inc.
San Diego, California 92111.

Second Edition
Copyright by Rachel Nutter
December 2007

ISBN: 978-0-595-50648-4 (pbk)
ISBN: 978-0-595-61596-4 (ebk)

Printed in the United States of America

To

    My five sons,

        My grandchildren

            My future great grandchildren

TABLE OF CONTENTS

Acknowledgements

*W*hen our children were very young, my husband suggested that I keep track of our family's precious moments. I've been tucking notes into a binder ever since.

When we were blessed with grandchildren, I decided to turn my shabby scraps of paper into this book. After I went through our photo albums and read scores of assorted notes and letters, the task I'd set for myself seemed truly daunting. But my "research" brought back many cherished memories and strengthened my resolve to give my family a unique gift. The process has been intensely personal and sometimes difficult, but it has been well worth all the effort.

When I began writing in earnest, I realized I needed help. These people are my contributors to this book and I give considerable credit for their help and generosity. A simple thank you does not convey a sufficient degree of indebtedness. My gratitude cannot be sufficiently measured because it is endless.

Carl McColman in Georgia was a man who gave me encouragement, constructive criticism and his words of inspiration always kept me on the right track

My five sons' love and encouragement, suggestions, and explanation with this endeavor have kept me searching for a better and significant approach to deliver this story in its true form.

To my son Terry, writer and editor: Your patience and your contributions during the early and final stages of this manuscript who has guided me and kept me searching for the right words.

To Willard and Isabelle Ayers, who touched our lives with their love and generosity during our growing years, I shall be eternally grateful.

To Ed and Marjorie Rodgers, who allowed our family the pure pleasure of sharing their dream, we are all so grateful. You touched our lives in countless loving ways.

To Vera Scheidt, Jack's secretary and longtime friend: I thank you for giving this manuscript a particularly sensitive reading. Your encouragement, kind thoughts, and genuine interest in this project have been so appreciated.

To my abiding friend Ruby Kane who offered succor and tolerance to me every step of the way has been a true blessing. Her advice has been a true force in getting things done. Her genuine interest and her contributions to helping me make this book a reality have been a pleasure and a privilege.

To Annabel Fogel of Chrysalis Editorial Services: I thank you for your guidance, your patience and your friendship.

This is a personal memoir, a gift to my family and friends and my future great-grandchildren. It's also a true love story: the love of my husband and the love of my five sons have been my greatest blessing in my entire life.

Foreword

*T*his story is about my five sons and my husband, who made me what I am today. It's also a story about my parents whose love and devotion to each other and love of God propelled me on to the same good and useful life. They set the stage; I only followed in their footsteps with pride, love of God, and the country I so dearly love.

The place of my birth was Denver, Colorado, on February 4, 1925. My wonderful Catholic parents were of limited income but we were a happy family of five who attended church regularly. I was enrolled at Annunciation Grammar School in Denver, Colorado and made my first Holy Communion in the second grade. To Mother and Dad, that was a great achievement, in view of the fact that they were never given the opportunity to attend school. They were born in the small town of Trinidad, Colorado, in 1907 and 1905 respectively.

Dad had a Model T truck that he used in the lettuce fields, making deliveries to small grocery stores in the area. In 1929 after the country plunged into economic depression my father lost his faith in banks and hid his cash in paper bags around the house. It was Mother, whose faith in God helped my father toss aside his banking fears.

Our evening church sessions would bring us home late, and Dad insisted we take off our shoes when we got out of the car so the clicking of our heels on the sidewalk wouldn't disturb our neighbors. His consideration of others always impressed me.

In 1936 my father moved his family to Los Angeles, California—with no job or a place to live. He felt California would give him a better opportunity to advance himself. Hard times persisted until Dad found a job that gave him a sense of pride and gave us financial security: he opened his own car wash business. Mother became his personal secretary and they opened their first bank account in 1939. As the years rolled by, their love for each other and of God always made us feel safe.

Early on I attended tap dancing school, but that was short-lived because of the expense. Dancing was natural to me. I learned a lot just by watching Eleanor Powell and Ginger Rogers. Gene Kelly's shadow dance in *Cover Girl* inspired me to dance in the middle of the street to my heart's content. Kelly and Fred Astaire were my idols.

Meeting the love of my life, Jack Nutter, gave me a different perspective. We had long talks about our future together. I grew up Catholic, where-as Jack was raised with no religion. We agreed to educate our children in my faith. Jack was very supportive and he felt privileged attending church with us.

When our sons were very young I sang and danced for them before they went to sleep. Jack had such a great voice that we often sang together for the boys.

The Year 1929

**Left to right on *Dad's* *Ford* *Truck*
in
Trinidad *Colorado*
Helen Abeyta Baby sister in buggy (six months.)
Rachel E. Abeyta On the hood "Me" (4 years.)
Edward R. Abeyta On the fender brother (5 years.)**

The 1929 "*Stock Market Crash*" when men were jumping out of buildings because all their savings were gone. Dad was delivering lettuce to local stores in the area from his truck in order to keep his family fed and healthy.

Chapter 1

It All Started at the USO

 $\mathcal{M}$ y story begins in January, 1945. For four long years, the country had been in the grip of war and life was anything but normal. I was twenty years old and doing my part for the war effort as a USO Volunteer. Two other girls and I had formed a trio and we helped to entertain the soldiers by singing popular songs. We weren't the Andrews Sisters, but we were pretty good.

Belonging to the USO was a special treat because we felt we were doing something important. Our soldiers were doing what their country asked of them, and they deserved our help. Traveling to the military bases and being involved in the entertainment field was fun, too.

When asked by our USO organizer, we'd travel on a Greyhound bus with other volunteers, usually for the weekend, to one of the many bases in central or southern California. When our turn came, my two friends and I would go up on the stage and perform our numbers. The rest of the time we either helped out with the many things that needed to be done or hung around the dance floor. Our volunteer work included accepting invitations to dance with the servicemen.

On one special night my group was scheduled to go to Camp Cook, two hours north of Los Angeles in San Bernardino County. We were to entertain Army servicemen just back from the thick of the action in Europe. After a few weeks of rest and recuperation, these soldiers would be boarding a ship headed for Europe again. One of the servicemen there that night was Private First Class Jack Nutter. I preferred tall men, and by the time I joined the USO I had already had boyfriends who were tall and very good-looking. Jack was only five foot seven (still, seven inches taller than me), he was very good-looking and I was to discover that he had a terrific personality.

After my friends and I had performed our numbers on stage, we left the stage and stood near the dance floor. I noticed one serviceman seemed to be doing a lot of looking around but not much dancing. A lot of the guys had no idea what dancing was about, and I wondered if he was one of them. He seemed to be looking at me, though every time I glanced over at him, he seemed to intentionally look away. I danced with a couple of the boys, and then after a long time, he came up to me and said, "May I have this dance?" "Can you dance?" I asked. "A little bit," he replied, "but I'm a fast learner."

I thought, "Not another one of those!" But I was obliged to dance with him, so I said OK and we went out onto the dance floor. He started off pretty slow with only a couple of steps. He kept that up for the rest of the number, only occasionally showing a little promise and then asking me if he was doing OK. I smiled and said yes. As the music played, we continued to dance. He said he thought he'd gotten the hang of it, and then I found out he really knew how to cut a rug! I loved to dance, and we ended up enjoying several dances that night.

Jack and I hit it off pretty well. Later that evening, he said he'd like to come to Los Angeles on weekend leave and take me somewhere. He asked for my number. My father was strict and didn't like us to have a lot of visitors. So, nonchalantly, I said, "Well, if you want to call me, my telephone number is in the book." I could see that he wasn't the least bit impressed. I didn't think he'd actually look up my number—but he did.

After that night at Camp Cook we dated three weekends in a row, going to the movies, to dinner, or to the Palladium, the large dance hall in L.A. America was at war and everyone's lives were affected by it. I think that helped make these weekends something special. After all, Jack was going back to the fighting in a few weeks. Who could say what would happen?

For those weekends, Jack traveled between Camp Cook and Los Angeles, where I lived, by Greyhound bus. My dad and I would pick him up at the downtown bus terminal and drive him to our house. From there we'd go out, traveling by bus or streetcar—

and we had a great time together. He was so easy to talk to and fun to be with.

Jack was from Concordia, Kansas. One evening at the Palladium, Jack told me he was going home to spend some time with his dad before going overseas again. He said when he got back from Kansas we'd get to see more of each other before he had to leave. This soldier seemed very sure of my willingness to see him. Well, maybe it was obvious! I suspected he only wanted to see me so he'd have a place to stay when he got back to L.A., so we said our goodbyes and that was the end of that, as far as I was concerned. Life went on and the days slipped by.

One evening a couple of weeks later, the telephone rang. Mother answered it, and she seemed to be having difficulty understanding just exactly who it was at the other end of the line. I thought she was acting a little strangely, so I asked her who was calling. As she looked at me she widened her eyes, blinked several times, and grinned. "It's Jack," she said.

"Jack who?" I really had begun to put him out of my mind. She covered the phone and said, "You know, the kid from Kansas." "Kansas?" I shouted. I'd liked him more than I had been willing to admit, and my suspicions had been completely unfounded. I eagerly grabbed the phone.

Jack was calling from Kansas. He said he had to report directly back to Camp Cook, but on the weekend he'd come to L.A. and we could go to dinner and then to a movie. Jack was as confident as they come; he didn't ask me if I wanted to go, he merely told me. His words were music to my ears, and so I said, "Sure, why not?"

That weekend, we went to dinner and enjoyed a great meal. Afterwards, he presented me with a lovely new glass jewel box containing a beautiful string of pearls. They were imitation, but that did not matter. I still have them to this day, and they are priceless.

On May 7, 1945, Germany surrendered and the war in Europe was over. It seemed as though everyone in America broke out in music dancing and celebration. Jack's life would now take a decisive turn. The military didn't need him anymore and he was elated at the prospect of getting out of the Army. The procedure and paperwork were rather lengthy and took time, but it finally happened. On his release, he came to Los Angeles again and Dad and I picked him up from the Greyhound depot for the last time. From that day forward Jack never uttered one word of his experiences about the war in Europe, other than having possessed a beautiful Lion Head Sword with *ruby eyes* and his German Luger (automatic pistol) that he managed to lift from a deceased German Officer. Those two items were his proudest possessions.

I hardly recognized him in his civilian clothes. He looked so different. Frankly, I liked him in his uniform. Jack was so happy to be free of the Army and out of that uniform that he could hardly contain himself. When we'd spoken on the phone, he'd said that he owned only one set of clothes and would need to do some shopping. My dad had decided to buy Jack some new clothes so on his arrival he announced to him that we were going to take him shopping. Jack, surprised, pointed uncertainly at himself. "Yes you!" Dad said.

We went downtown and spent the next few hours shopping strictly for him. Dad bought Jack a suit, shirt, tie, shoes, and socks—a complete set of new clothing! For my father, who would rarely reach into his pocket for money, this behavior was uncharacteristically generous and this suggested to me that he really liked Jack. Jack was so pleased he kept thanking him.

Jack moved in with his older brother, Mac, near the beach in Santa Monica and began looking for work. He also sent applications to several universities to study law. A lot of other ex-soldiers were flooding the market and jobs were scarce. Finally, after two months, Jack got a low-paying job with the Curtis Watch Hospital on Santa Monica Boulevard. At least he had work.

After we'd dated for five months, Jack asked me to marry him. I was elated, and we began making plans. When we told my parents, they tried to talk us out of it because they felt we should spend more time getting to know each other before we tied ourselves down.

Without saying anything to my parents, Jack and I went to see Father Karl at Sacred Heart Church in Los Angeles. Wouldn't you know it—Father Karl tried to talk us into waiting at least a year! Jack listened very patiently, then said, "I'm sorry, Father, but no. We either get married here in the church as we plan to do, or we'll go to Las Vegas and get married by a Justice of the Peace."

"Not so fast," protested Father Karl, and then, taking Jack's determination into consideration, he relented. He got out his book and wrote down our names and the date we had set for our wedding.

Father Karl knew Jack didn't observe religious traditions, and he recommended that Jack take lessons before our wedding in the Catholic Church. Jack listened ever so patiently, and agreed. Without the slightest complaint, he faithfully attended each lesson.

Before the wedding, Jack's mother, Doris Nutter, flew in from Kansas to meet me along with my Mother and Dad. Jack told me that she had left his father, McKinley, and their three sons because she got tired of cooking for everyone who worked on their wheat farm. She moved to Belleville, where she drove a school bus. After that she moved and changed jobs several times. I imagined that Doris was a high-spirited, independent woman, and that we'd become fast friends. I was wrong. When she learned I was of the Catholic faith she was absolutely infuriated, and demanded that Jack explain why he "had to marry a Catholic girl." That was very painful for all of us, but I reasoned that Doris would come around once she knew me better and realized how happy her son was.

Finally, that once-in-a-lifetime day dawned. I couldn't believe it was actually happening. Both our lives were now taking another decisive turn. If there'd been any career in my future, I threw it out the window at my wedding. Thankfully, my parents' feelings about Jack and our ignoring their advice eventually mellowed into a beautiful love for him.

On April 6, 1946, my father escorted me down the aisle. Father Russell T. Karl married us at the Sacred Heart Church in Los Angeles, California. Jack's older brother Mac was his best man, and my only sister, Helen, was my matron of honor.

I'd always believed that my wedding day would be a perfect fairy-tale experience, something I'd cherish in my heart for the rest of my life. The church's organist had forgotten about my big moment! She left me waiting—not at the altar, but at the back of the church. No wedding march? I couldn't imagine it. But when we'd waited as long as we could, finally my Dad and I started down the aisle. The silence was so awkward; it felt like I was getting married in a library!

My father was terribly irritated. As he and I stumbled down the aisle he kept whispering in my ear (and not too softly, mind you),

"Is this really happening to us? Have you ever heard of such a thing? This is terrible!" I kept trying to shush him, but he ignored me. As we walked mostly in silence down that aisle, some of our guests glanced up at the loft where the organ was. I wondered how my perfect plans could go so wrong. I felt so bad I began asking myself what am I doing here?

Then I looked up at my bridegroom with a big smile on his face and I forgot all about the silence. We were both so happy our wedding was finally coming to the end. The planning, the invitations, the ordering of the flowers and all the other details finally had come together and we only had a few more moments to go. There'd be no more long trips on the streetcar to Santa Monica to Mac's place, where Jack had been living. Soon we'd be husband and wife.

As my father handed me over to my husband, they smiled at each other. Then Jack leaned over and whispered that the music wasn't all that important. He squeezed my hand and gave me a reassuring smile and a double wink. I suddenly felt relieved, and much better about everything.

Father Karl married us, and then congratulated us with a firm handshake each. Then he quietly apologized about the absence of the organist. Jack assured Father it was nothing to worry about.

What a way to get started! Emerging from the cathedral with my husband, gave us both the greatest feeling of love for each other. Afterwards on to my parents' home for the reception.

We were unable to afford a honeymoon, so after the reception we headed for our new home in Santa Monica. We called it our shack. Jack had signed the rental agreement the day before we were married. It was a single room in a house on 6th Street that had been converted into a rooming house. Mercy, this house was so shabby and dilapidated it had to be at least a hundred years old, but at that time apartment rentals were unheard of. Our room was upstairs, the kitchen downstairs. We shared the kitchen and bath with all the other renters. An unpainted wooden staircase outside the building was the only access to our room. It wasn't what you'd call the honeymoon suite, but it was a roof over our heads. As we settled in and gazed around the room, my new husband hugged me and said, "Stick with me, kid, and you'll be wearing diamonds and mink before you know it!"

Just a few days after our wedding Jack wanted to go to the beach. I made a special effort to get ready fast, and in my haste I left my wedding rings on the tub in the bathroom. While we were walking in the sand I realized the absence of my rings. In panic, we both ran back to the house. I could not keep up with Jack and as I approached the back yard, Jack was coming down the wooden stairs shaking his head. The rings were gone. We tried to notify all the patrons at the house, but no one responded to the loss. I was heart broken. We could not afford another ring so I purchased a dime store gold band for ten cents. It was terrible.

One Saturday afternoon while he was at work, I decided to bake Jack a cake. I'd tried before without much luck, but this time everything went well; the frosted cake looked great, and I felt proud of my achievement. As I carried it up the old wooden staircase, imagining how surprised and pleased Jack would be, I missed a step and fell. I tried to protect the cake as I hit the next step but only partially succeeded. My first cake, and what a mess! I patched it up as well as I could, but since it was chocolate with chocolate frosting, it look like one of those mud pies I used to make when I was little. I was as crestfallen as my poor cake.

When Jack got home I set our meal before him on our make-shift table. He complimented me about the table setting and ate heartily. "This is really delicious!" he said. "Your mother taught you well." I felt awful because the meal wasn't that good, but I accepted his compliments. When we'd finished eating, I reluctantly brought out the cake and cut a piece for him. He stared at it open-mouthed, fork in hand and pure amazement on his face. It looked terrible, but I said, "This is what I call the ideal and fitting end to an enjoyable meal. It's not only delicious, but beautiful as well."

I was dying inside, but he forced a smile and dug in without a word. He made a nice little noise like "hum" as he crunched on what I believed was dirt from the step, but he acted like he was enjoying himself and I didn't want to spoil it. When he said, "Delicious; you must do this again," then and only then could I laugh and tell him what truly took place. He laughed with me and then said, "Looks terrible, honey, but it really is good."

Before we were married, I'd worked as a switchboard operator for Crook Co., a large L.A. business that leased heavy construction equipment. During the week, I had to get up early and make a long commute on the bus to get to work by 7:30 A.M. The hours were just too long, so I thought about returning to my old job as a telephone company traffic operator. There was an exchange only four blocks from our shack, so one day I dropped by and filled out an application.

It was just after this that I broke the news to Jack that I was pregnant. We were both very excited. "What would you like," I asked, "a boy or a girl?" "A healthy baby makes no difference to me," he said. I wanted a little girl, but I felt the same about the baby's health. Soon after this, morning sickness began to hit me every day at seven, turning my long morning commute into a nightmare. Jack and I were wondering what to do when, fortunately, the telephone company called to say I'd been rehired. I had to start my day at six, get my morning sickness over with, and get to work by nine. It was awful, but it worked.

With a family on the way, we needed a car. Jack looked around and found a dream car: a blue Ford Sedan, only eleven years old. Dad felt that we should pick out a name for this poor excuse of a vehicle, (kind of silly) so we called her Henrietta. She was missing a cog on the starter flywheel. If the starter stopped on that missing cog, Jack usually had to raise the hood, remove the starter, and turn the wheel past the missing gap to start her again. This happened a lot, especially when Jack was dressed for work in his white shirt and tie. What a pain! But at least now we could get to the hospital on our own when the baby decided to arrive.

This car also leaked through the roof. The windshield was designed to be pushed up and out in order to allow lots of fresh air into the car when necessary. When the wind hit the windshield just right, it usually showered us with rain or swirls of dust. It was hilarious the first few times. I loved that car, but I hated it too.

Jack and I thought about names for our baby. I took to knitting and crocheting special things for a little girl just in case we were lucky to start with a daughter. If she turned out to be a he, without telling Jack, I decided on two names. It would be Jacqueline for a little girl, or he would be Jack. Either way, our baby would be named after its father. In those days, only at the birth of the baby would we know what the sex would be, so our plans for clothing had to fit both.

8

Chapter 2

And Baby Makes Three

*E*arly on the morning of Tuesday, February 25, 1947, my dear but nervous husband rushed me to the Queen of Angeles Hospital in Los Angeles. Jack seemed to be trying to shorten the long drive from Santa Monica. I was afraid we were going to have an accident, but I stoically told him I was fine and to be careful. With nervous excitement, we finally pulled up at the hospital and I was taken to the delivery room. Jack was relegated to the waiting room with all the other expectant fathers.

In the early morning hours our first son emerged, making us a complete family. Jackie balanced the scales at 7 pounds 14 ounces, stretched out to 21 inches, and had a mop of fine, thick, long black hair. When the doctor complimented us on our beautiful son, Jack told him the baby needed a haircut before we took him home. It was true; Jackie's ebony hair fell to his shoulders. It was so fine I could hardly feel it. I would roll it around two fingers and make a curl on top of his head.

The next day I was told that after the birth my blood wouldn't coagulate a serious problem since there were no drugs that could help me. The doctor's decision might have serious consequences. What could he do? Finally, he stuffed my uterus with yards and yards of gauze in order to stop the hemorrhage. To his relief—and mine!—The bleeding stopped, and I was assured a complete recovery.

Jack was anxious to send out birth announcements while I recuperated. He called me at the hospital to ask what name I'd chosen for the baby. When I told him Jack Jr., he asked if I was sure. "Positive," I said. Jack was thrilled and delighted. He bought beautiful cards to announce our baby's birth, filled in the details, and mailed them the following evening. When he told me what he'd done, I realized just how excited he was about the arrival of our first born.

On my second day in the hospital my dear friend Jane Curly came to visit, bringing me flowers and a gift. She hugged me with the endearing words, "*Welcome to this wonderful world of motherhood!*" I opened the box and there lay a beautiful Kelly green dress she'd made especially for me. I was so thrilled of her thoughtfulness I wore this dress proudly on many special occasions over the years. Jane was a fine seamstress; she taught me how to sew and read patterns, enabling me to design my own clothes for many years to come. She was a very special friend.

Early Sunday morning one of the Sisters came to tell me that they were ready to do Jackie's birth certificate. When she asked for his full name, I proudly said, "Jack Wilcox Nutter, Junior." She smilingly wrote the name in her notepad and then applied my thumbprints to the birth certificate. She explained that the certificate would be waiting for us on our departure from the hospital.

On the appointed day, Jack and my Dad came to take us home. First he had to pay for the remaining debt to the hospital, which was $50.00. Then Jack went to fetch the most beautiful birth certificate I've ever seen: the design was quite ornate, the details were written in beautiful script, and my thumbprints and Jackie's footprints were clearly distinguished. But there was a flaw. Only after I accepted it did I discover that they'd replaced "Jack" with "John." I was furious and insisted the error be corrected. It took time, and the hospital registrar wasn't happy about it, but our son bore his father's name I wanted it to remain as such. Before long we finally waved goodbye to the hospital staff. We stayed at my parents' home in West L.A. for a few days before Jack drove the three of us home to our shack in Santa Monica.

Soon baby gifts began flooding in from everyone we knew. Our most cherished gift was a very useful *Thayer Baby Table* with an inserted seat. As soon as Jackie was able to sit up I could set him in the seat to feed him. The table was large enough for his toys and he could sit in the seat and play. Thayer was practical and extremely useful for many years.

Jack was so happy with Jackie. I found him rocking him to sleep every night. If he didn't go to sleep right away he would lay him on his chest and pat his back until the both of them were asleep. That created a serious problem because our young son would not accept his crib at night after that. He wanted his dad to cradle him.

Two months later, Jackie was baptized and his grandparents did the honors as godparents. It was a very special occasion. Our first-born was my Mother and Dad's first grandchild and they adored him. Mother bought his outfit and she herself dressed Jackie that Sunday morning before we headed for the church.

Five months later, I took Jackie to a photographer. His portrait was absolutely priceless, and everyone in the family received a print. My parents displayed Jackie's picture over their fireplace. His smile alone would capture your heart.

When Jackie was a year old, the *Gerber Company* held a baby contest in Santa Monica, California. My son's personality and his beautiful smile won people's hearts everywhere we went, and I thought this contest would be an cinch for him to win.

As the contest approached, I filled out all the necessary paper work. After some thought, I bought him a beautiful white sun suit with a matching hat and shoes. With his dark hair, sparkling eyes, and charming smile he was beautiful in his new outfit. On the day of the contest, Jackie had smiles and a big bubbly "Hi" for every-one at the bus stop; he'd also fan his hand and wave hello to them. As we rode the bus, I could imagine all the Gerber advertisements in the papers featuring my beautiful son, nothing less than the new *"Gerber Baby."* What a dreamer I was.

When we arrived at the auditorium there were mothers and babies everywhere. I realized then that it wasn't going to be easy for Jackie to become the Gerber Baby. But I was positive that his personality, beautiful smile, and quaint little actions would win the judges' hearts. I decided not to worry.

We mothers were directed to form a line and stand our babies on a long table in front of ten different judges. As my turn came up, I handed my application to the first judge. She talked to Jackie, remarked about his outfit, she tickled his knees, his chin and tugged at his shirt. She tried everything to make him smile, but absolutely nothing came out of Jackie. The judge then put a mark on my paperwork and passed it to the second judge. Again, Jackie simply wasn't interested. He was as serious as he could be;

not even a hint of a smile, nor any of his spectacular fanfare with his head or hands. I couldn't believe it. He did nothing as we went through all ten judges. Jackie watched the babies before him and behind him, but he didn't care. I tried to get him to wave good-bye, anything, but he just stood there as serious as a little judge himself.

As the last judge reviewed my application, she saw no significant points of interest for my son. Like the others, she made a funny face for him, but there was no response. She checked my paperwork again, returned it to me and said, "Your son has beautiful eyes, and his outfit is priceless; perhaps you might want to enter him in our next contest." Not the least bit sure how to take that. I was crushed. Why couldn't he show them he'd make the perfect Gerber Baby? I sadly lifted my son in my arms and said, "Thank you, but no thanks."

The judge smiled sympathetically. "I'm sorry," she said. I hugged my son as I walked away fighting back the tears. I said to my son, "Honey, how could you?" Jackie just looked at me with a questioning kind of expression. Could he be wondering what I was talking about, or why the tears in my eyes?

As I carried him to the bus stop he kept looking at me with that puzzled expression. I decided not to make him feel bad; after all, it wasn't his fault, he was just a baby. I stood Jackie on the bench while we waited for the bus. My son flirted with everyone at that bus stop! He stooped over and said "Hi" with his little head upside down, his hands on his knees for balance. When he got no response from those he greeted, he did it again and again. He'd wave his hands and tip his head in the cutest gesture. He was determined to get a reaction. As we boarded the bus, Jackie greeted the driver with a great big "Hi" and a big smile. He received a loud, *"Hi there, young man!"* in return. Jackie turned to me with one of his big, approving smiles. If only those judges could have seen him at that bus stop!

When Jack came home that evening and heard my story about our day at the contest, he laughed, picked Jackie up and said, "That's OK, son, we understand." Then he looked at me, and added, "Right, Mom?"

Our first son was a delight. Even though he wasn't talking yet, he was very bright and he seemed to understand everything that was going on. He was very obedient. In fact, I never had to speak to him twice. If I felt any disapproval for what he was doing, all I had to do was shake my head and he'd stop, correct whatever he'd done, and go on to something else.

When he'd notice me watching him he'd smile that bewitching smile. His teeth were perfect. His complexion was clear with a somewhat olive tint. His big, brown, sparkling eyes were so lovely they complemented his pleasant, cheerful personality. All these things won compliments wherever we went.

He had a million-dollar smile and a personality to go with it—and still does. Thank you, God! I couldn't have asked for more.

Taken in front of the "Golden Stairs" (our little shack) a week after our wedding. My first attempt on baking a cake ended up on these steps.

Mr. & Mrs. J. W. Nutter
April 14, 1946
Santa Monica, California

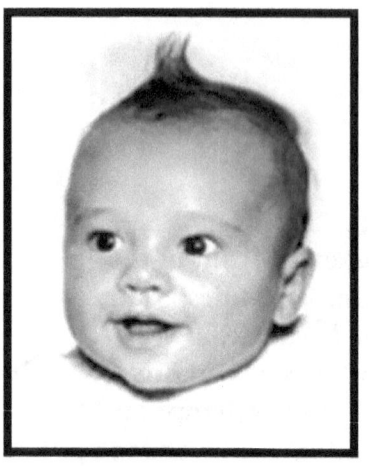

**Jack W. Nutter Jr.
Eleven Months
Entered "Gerbers Baby Contest."
Santa Monica, California 1947
Jackie was not impressed with this
Contest and he was not influenced
By the Judges.**

**Jackie Nutter in his new suit with Grandpa Abeyta and first
cousin Edward Abeyta**

Jackie's first outing at San Juan Capistrano with Dad and Mom
Age three months

The opening arch at San Juan Capistrano with Dad and Jackie

Chapter 3

Second Son, Second Home

*O*ur tiny "shack" was much too small for another addition to our growing family. House rentals were still out of the question, so we decided to see what was out there. Jack found a rather unusual but prominent ad in the Sunday paper which read: "Elderly school teacher willing to rent sleeping quarters with kitchen privileges to a young couple in Santa Monica. Requirement: must be a World War II Veteran." Jack said, "Honey we qualify for this!"

Immediately we made the call and this lady (Mrs. Walsh) was most endearing, and she liked both of us. That same afternoon we rented a room in her beautiful residence at 915 Georgina, Santa Monica, California. We were honored to be able to live in her home, even if only for a year or two. Another veteran couple occupied the second bedroom making the house complete. It was great.

On Tuesday, March 12, 1948, at 10:15 P.M. Patrick James Nutter made our family a foursome at Santa Monica Hospital. He weighed in at 7 pounds 10 ounces, and stretched out to 20 inches. He had blond, slightly curly peach fuzz for hair. Again, I had hoped to have a girl, even going so far as to pick the name Patricia. And for the second time, I had a precious boy instead.

Our priceless son had very dry skin and the hospital kept him dipped in baby oil. When his father approached the nursery to view his second son, the nurse propped him up to show him at his best. Jack was disappointed; all he could see was wrinkles, and grease all over his face and arms. He left the nursery and walked to my room looking exhausted. He greeted me with a hug and a kiss. His first words to me about our new son were: "Honey, I hate to say this, but the baby is so wrinkled! Already he looks like a little old man." I laughed heartily at this; I knew Jack was used to Jackie's beautiful skin. I told him that a new baby's skin is altogether different. He simply had forgotten how Jackie looked when he first came home. Nevertheless, I was rather anxious to see for myself what a little old man looked like in such a short time!

A few hours later, when the nurse first presented Patrick to me, I couldn't see the wrinkles. His skin was dry and very soft. I cuddled him in my arms and told him what his father had said about him, but it didn't impress him in the least. Jack felt that if we fed Patrick all the milk he could drink, it would smooth all those creases. It was so funny.

I remained at the hospital the typical three days, and then Jack drove us to our new residence in Santa Monica. When Jack, Patrick and I got home we found my mother anxiously waiting for our new arrival. As Mother cradled Patrick in her arms her first comment was, "He's a carbon copy of his father." I couldn't see it at the time, but later I realized there was a great resemblance. I began using baby cream on him, and in a very short time we noticed that Patrick's skin was so clear that it looked like peaches and cream. His complexion was positively beautiful. His fuzzy hair became curly and blond, his eyes were brown, and his smile never failed to make me feel warm all over, toothless as he was.

Soon the hospital staff was ready to prepare Patrick's birth certificate. I had requested it upon our departure, but was told we needed to write the County Recorder's Office for it once we were home. When the certificate arrived in the mail it was a plain printed document, typed on a very poor typewriter. There was no comparison to Jackie's beautiful certificate. I was so disappointed.

Jackie couldn't take his eyes off the baby. He'd pat his cheek and kiss his forehead. At times he'd cup his hand and hold Patrick's cheeks and kiss him. He felt no jealousy for his little brother—or so I thought.

I kept Jackie busy handing me diapers and baby powder. On occasion, I even had him help me with his brother's bath. I talked to him constantly about his brother, explaining how he needed to help me take care of Patrick. I wanted to plant the idea of being responsible and caring, even though Jackie was just a year older than Patrick and still a baby himself.

Going shopping with the two boys proved to be quite a chore. My mother purchased a beautiful buggy for us, and with it I could trot down to the store with both babies. As Jackie rode with Patrick, he'd always point at his little brother when people admired them.

For Mother's Day that year Jack took Jackie shopping with him and they surprised me with a demitasse tea set for six from Germany. Jack signed a special card from "Jackie, Patrick, and me." I've kept the tea set for use on special occasions, and it remains one of my most cherished possessions.

Uncle Leo and Aunt Margaret, my dad's brother and his wife, wanted to be Patrick's godparents and I appreciated the idea. So Jack and I made plans to have Patrick baptized in June at Sacred Heart Church. No need for the organ this time, (Ha) and we used Jackie's baptismal outfit.

During those early years Jack worked in a jewelry store in Santa Monica. He was being paid for learning the trade while working on the job, and the Federal Veterans' Administration subsidized his salary. With our young family, it became impossible to meet the cost of living on Jack's $25-a-week salary and $60-a-month subsidy. (a government grant.) He needed work with substantial take-home pay.

An Army buddy of Jack's realized our problem, and recommended a small company that was just coming into its own. Even though Jack knew nothing about the business, he still saw it as a great opportunity. The job not only paid well, it carried more prestige than a retail clerk in a jewelry store. It also seemed to have potential for future growth. Jack felt a strong desire to learn, so he called the company's president and set up an interview.

Davre Davidson, president of the Culver City—based company, otherwise known as "Davidson Brothers" conducted the interview and it went well. Jack was promised, in addition to his salary, medical insurance for our family of four as well as retirement benefits, making this position far superior to that of the jewelry store clerk. Granted, it demanded devotion, hard work, and concentration on the company's growth, but Jack found these demands exciting. His personality and his eagerness to excel were inspiring. He was very responsible and in a very short time he helped the company grow much faster than anticipated. Jack grew mentally, spiritually, and financially. God was with him and I was ever so proud of him.

Mr. Davidson's company distributed cigarette vending machines to local businesses. Back then, society did not worry about the health risks associated with tobacco; in fact, cigarette companies ran ads in which doctors endorsed their products! Our evening ritual after dinner Jack would take the both of us in the car with him to canvas the neighborhood for different locations in order to place the company's vending machines. To him this was an indication that I approved this late hour ritual. I really didn't, but I did not want to discourage him. Jack never questioned the product he sold. Of course, when he understood years later that many health risks are associated with tobacco, it did bother him. But the career choice he made in the '40s was based on the belief, common at that time, that cigarettes were not a health hazard. Live and Learn.

After Jack changed jobs, the government continued sending us those monthly $60 checks. I wrote a letter explaining that Jack no longer was attending school, but the checks continued for one full year. We knew we'd have to return them, so we kept them in a safe place. One day we heard from the Veterans' Administration: a Notice of Interruption of Education. Their office had been informed that Jack had interrupted his course of education under the provisions of Public Law 346. His award of subsistence allowance had been terminated. We were requested to meet with a Mr. Lyons at the Veterans' Administration in West L.A. the following week.

Mr. Lyons was very cordial and asked Jack if he wanted to re-enter the same school or firm. "Not at this time," Jack answered. "In that case, Mr. Nutter, you owe the government a total of $750.00." Mr. Lyons then asked. "When would you be able to start making payments?" Jack then reached into his vest pocket and he spread all the checks on his desk. "Mr. Lyons, these are all the checks that were sent to us." The expression on the man's face was one of total amazement. "I didn't …" he began, but Jack interrupted him, saying, "If our business is completed, sir, we'd like a receipt so that we may be on our way." "Of course," replied the shaken Mr. Lyons. He wrote out a receipt, and we proudly left his office. Jack had a smile on his face a mile long. He was so proud of himself.

Since I had been giving so much attention to Patrick, I discovered that Jackie was getting lazy about talking. Pat didn't talk, so why should he? I understood him, so nothing else mattered. I felt that he'd talk when he was ready, so I didn't push. He saw to it that Patrick got his bottle when he cried and he would not let me rest if he thought Patrick was wet. During play Jackie would hide from his brother, and then suddenly reappear. Patrick's eyes would get wide, his arms would fly the air, and the roar of laughter that came out of his mouth was music to my ears. Big brother's attention was always in demand.

Doris, Jack's mother, was partial to Patrick. He was so beautiful and endearing. I'm not sure why I didn't think of entering him in a baby contest. After all, Patrick surely would have shown those judges a thing or two. I know that I would've trained him differently. I took too much for granted with Jackie, as most mothers do with their first-born. At any rate, with two boys less than two years old I had no time to even think about a contest.

Grandma Doris would come over often enough to spoil both boys. I loved the attention she gave them. It would take the pressure off me and give me time to relax, while at the same time keep Doris busy. I always made it a point to thank the boys for the little things they did during the day and I would thank her for her help. The boys were babies but they were very sharp. Jack and I never used baby talk with our boys. We wanted them to have a good vocabulary and I always corrected my sons whenever they acted inappropriately. Luckily for me, they responded to my discipline. I was really lucky, they were such a joy!

Our Santa Monica home was nine blocks from the beach and exceptionally beautiful. Even with Jack's new job, new housing was still unheard of; we therefore decided to look for a house to rent. Patrick was starting to climb and getting into everything, and Jackie's endless energy made me worry about everybody's personal belongings in that house. It was time for us to move again.

We found a little duplex in Mar Vista with two bedrooms, a large living room, and an oblong kitchen with one bath. A short white fence surrounded the yard. It was exactly what we needed. Rent was $50 a month, which we considered an outrageous price, but we desperately needed the duplex. Our total belongings, clothing and the like, along with our two boys and the car, were all Jack and I had in the world.

The only furniture we had was the boys' little Thayer table, the bed, and the buggy. With no furniture we needed to do something fast. We scanned the newspaper for necessities.

Dad found a used couch with sprung springs that Jack felt we could use for the time being. It looked like it belonged in the trash, but the boys could never damage it, for it was built like the Rock of Gibraltar. It cost $10, and what a buy! We also found a small icebox that held only a 25-pound block of ice. On cool days the ice would last about three weeks; in hot weather, about two weeks. I had to look under the ice compartment constantly for dripping ice water. If I didn't catch it in time the tray would run over and I'd have a total mess to clean—as happened on many occasions!

All our relatives wanted to visit us in our little house one Sunday. We had no furniture other than the bedroom set I'd used as a teenager and a new floor lamp for our living room, all gifts from my parents, so Jack and his brother set out one Sunday morning to find something. Two hours later they showed up with four wooden orange crates and a card table. I didn't know whether to laugh or cry! Covering the crates with towels made them more presentable, and later that afternoon our guests made no mention of our makeshift furniture. A friend of Jack's gave him a chair with wooden arms, and we set it alongside Mother and Dad's lamp. Jackie thought the orange crates were fabulous. He could run his little cars in and out of them easily, and it was fun for him and easy to entertain himself.

One evening I informed Jack that I needed things at the drug store. Go ahead Mom; I'll care for our two boys. While I was gone Jack sat in the chair given by his friend, reading the evening paper with Jackie on his lap. Jackie was in training pants, and when nature called, he tried to get his father's attention. Jack, as usual, was so engrossed in his paper that he ignored his son. Our son, who never liked to be dirty, dealt with the situation the only way he knew how—by reaching into the leg of his pants, pulling out the mess, spreading it all over the arm of the chair, and wiping his hands on his father's arm. Finally Jack's nose picked up a strong odor; he looked down, jumped to his feet as he dropped the paper and raced Jackie to the bathroom. He sat Jackie in the tub while he soaped his arm. When I got home Jack was mumbling and grumbling as he tried to clean the arm of the chair. As he told me the story, I went into the bedroom and had a good laugh—and allowed him to continue cleaning. Then I told him, "Next time, you will know that you need to pay more attention to your son." "Right?" "Thanks for nothing Mom, Thanks!"

Chapter 4

Our Third Baby Boomer

*T*hree months after Patrick's birth, I announced to my husband and my mother that our third baby was on its way. Preparing for the arrival of a new baby was no problem. At this point we had plenty of space for growth in the little duplex, and there were plenty of baby clothes. Again hoping for a girl, I started to crochet Afghans, bonnets, and matching booties. I used different styles and colors because I wanted something different this time; being partial to yellow, I concentrated on white and yellow combinations. A companionable name for a little girl seemed very important, and so I decided on Theresa. I'd give Jack the opportunity to pick out the middle name.

On Tuesday morning, May 3, 1949, Jack drove yours truly to St. John's Hospital in Santa Monica again. Our third son arrived at about 6:30 A.M. He weighed 7 pounds 8 ounces and stretched to 20 inches. He had a mop of black hair, straight and shiny, that stood up like a porcupine's quills.

The events in the hospital that morning seemed to blur. My first clear memory, after entering the delivery room, was of a nurse patting my cheek as I opened my eyes. Naturally, I reached for my stomach and thought I still was carrying the baby. I groaned when the nurse said, "The doctor had a very difficult time with your delivery, but everything is fine now." I had hemorrhaged again, and this time sand bags were placed on my stomach to stop the bleeding.

I felt weak and shaky, but no matter; all I wanted was to see the baby. The nurse told me I had a beautiful little boy with lots of black hair. "Another boy?" I said. "I already have two of them at home." She told me she'd bring my baby to me soon, but in the meantime I needed to be very still. Soon after the doctor informed me that I was in dire need of a blood transfusion and that he'd order the blood. After the transfusion the following day, I really felt much better. I was getting anxious to pick up the baby and go home. I was homesick.

This time Grandma Doris was caring for the boys in our Mar Vista residence, so I had nothing to worry about. Doris decided it was time for Jackie to start talking. She started him with small sentences as he pointed to various things he wanted. That kept both of them very busy. Jackie seemed to thrive on her attention and when Grandma wasn't talking to him, he'd tug at her dress, pointing to other things he wanted. She continued to explain the names of the things he asked for, giving him her undivided attention. Patrick was too young to do more than just listen and watch.

A couple of days later the nurse came to tell me that the baby's birth certificate was being prepared, and asked for the baby's name. I told her Terrill Mark Nutter, thinking that as he got older he could choose either name or Terry for short. I learned later that "Terrill" was already part of the Nutter family tree.

After four days in the hospital Jack came for us. He himself had picked out the clothes for his third son to wear home. Needless to say, he did not bring any of the little outfits I'd crocheted. On our departure all the nurses said to me, "See you next year." I thought, how crazy; three boys are enough for any mother!

When we arrived at our little duplex, Grandma was elated with our new son. Jackie and Patrick hugged and kissed the baby as he lay sleeping in my arms. I was exhausted, so Dad helped me into the bedroom. Jackie followed us with much enthusiasm, and he kept tugging at my arm as I was lying down. Finally I asked, "What is it, Jackie?" His eyes got as big as saucers and he said, "Da, da, tu, tu, twain wuns on da thwack."

I was so surprised to hear him talk, I said, "What did you say, Jackie?" He said it again with zest and pride. I pulled him close to me and I told him I loved it when he talked. He ran to his father and repeated the sentence. Jack said, "Wow, that's great son, but now it's time to let Mom rest. You go into the other room and look after Patrick." He hugged him and set him down. Jackie turned to me as he walked out waving goodbye. I said, "Aren't you forgetting something?" He ran to hug me and kiss me, and then walked away, waving and blowing more kisses. Jack said, "I have a feeling he's going to talk your head off from here on out."

He was so right! Jackie wanted to talk about everything he looked at, and now he had two brothers to entertain. He was getting to be a big boy, and wore training pants off and on. Just when I thought he was ready to get out of diapers entirely, he showed me he needed more attention.

Early one morning as I was bathing Terry, Jackie did everything he could to get my attention. He finally got it when I noticed him red in the face, mouth open, eyes fixed in a strange frown. I realized exactly what he was doing but couldn't control what happened next: his training pants dropped and along came a stream of you-know-what. I screamed, "Jackie, don't do it!" and with that he burst into tears. I hurried to finish Terry's bath, then cleaned up my oldest son and pinned a diaper on him.

I devoted the rest of the morning to playing with Jackie while talking to him almost constantly. I wanted to teach him more about helping me with Patrick and Terry, and how being productive helped all of us. He was a good listener, and loved the individual attention. As young as he was, he soon realized just how important he was to the family, and his attitude seemed to change.

A steady stream of relatives came to see the new baby. One of our most distinguished visitors was my paternal grandmother. My Aunt Margaret and Uncle Leo brought her over one Sunday afternoon. She was 79 years old at the time but looked every bit of 99. She'd had a very hard life and it showed. I handed Grandma the baby wrapped in a blanket and she held him ever so lightly. She kept repeating how little and beautiful he was, saying, "You must be very proud of him!" as she handed Terry back to me. Later in the week, Aunt Margaret called me to say that Grandma felt so sorry for me, when I asked why, Grandma said to Aunt Margaret "the baby never grows." It was then explained to her that Terry was a different baby.

Uncle Leo walked over to admire the baby as I stood next to Patrick, who was sitting in the Thayer table seat munching on crackers. I adjusted Terry's blanket for a better view, not realizing that his little foot was exposed. The temptation was too great for Patrick to pass up. Uncle Leo casually looked down and saw that Patrick had Terry's big toe in his mouth, ready to bite down. He gently grabbed Patrick from his table, releasing the toe from those sharp little teeth. Everybody laughed—more from relief than amusement.

Once again my Mother and Dad did the honors as godparents at Terry's christening. The same outfit that mother originally purchased for Jackie was worn for the third time. Terry, as usual, made no fuss about all that was going on around him. When the holy water was poured over his head, his eyes widened and he moved a little as he smiled at his godmother. After the ceremony, pictures were taken before Jackie and Patrick drove off with Grandma and Grandpa in their beautiful Cadillac. Our little Henrietta carried Jack, Terry, and me home to finish the festivities with the special meal that awaited us all. Three boys I said to myself. Please God help me.

The boys were infatuated with their baby bother; they'd sit on the bed just watching him sleep. With Terry's slightest move, they'd notify me that he was hungry. In their presence I'd pick him up, put his cheek next to mine, and rock him back and forth as I hummed a soft lullaby. Before we knew it he was sound asleep again. I'd return him to his bassinet as each boy kissed his cheek, and we'd all tiptoe out of the room. At seven months, Terry no longer required a bottle to fall asleep. A drink of milk from a cup, while standing in his crib, was all he needed. Down he'd go and almost immediately be sound asleep.

The two older boys were growing more athletic. While Jackie rode his tricycle up and down the cement walk, Patrick would climb the short fence in our front yard and hang from it, watching his brother and the passersby. His golden blond curls and his fancy stance on the fence made him seem even more priceless. Everyone who passed by took notice of him; saying "Isn't she beautiful?" His beautiful blond curls gave a female impression. Grandma Doris hated Pat's hair; she said he looked too much like a girl. She wanted to cut off his curls, but I remained persistent. "He's still a baby," I said. "I want to wait until absolutely necessary before I cut his hair." When she insisted, I'd resort to begging: "Please, Grandma, let me enjoy him like this a little longer."

After dinner one evening, our landlord dropped by our small residence to see us. He was very cordially thanked Jack for paying our rent on time. He went on to say that he felt three children in our little duplex was too much, and asked us to look for another place to live. I was furious about this sudden turn of events—after all, we'd been here such a short time—so I asked if we had created any problems for him or his wife. His first complaint was about Patrick. "When your son climbs the fence, it's bad for the wood." Jack and I were astounded. I asked if there were anything else. He nodded. "You use too much of the clothesline when you wash the boys' clothes. You leave my wife very little room for our clothes." I apologized. He asked us to please be out in thirty days. We agreed, and we were. That same day, all five of us set out to look for a place to rent.

It seemed that every time a baby was born, we had to move. The following week Jack called about a house at 1356 Felton Street in Inglewood. With very little furniture, we moved to our new home in one day. Even though it was right under the L.A. International Airport path, it was the answer to our prayers: two bedrooms, separate dining and living room, one bath, a nice kitchen, and a large, fenced yard. I was constantly straightening the pictures on the walls because of the vibration from planes flying overhead, but the house was great.

Jack's job was keeping him busy and he was working long hours every day. My schedule with the boys kept me busy from morning until late in the evening. Many times the boys would wrestle with their Dad just before they had their baths. After prayers we'd kiss each one good night and whisper sweet nothings in their ears. We always thanked them for their good deeds of the day. Before we knew it Mr. Sandman took over.

Sometimes when Jack came home he'd play his ukulele for the boys before bedtime. They loved to hear him sing and play "Home on the Range." When he finished they'd clap and say, "More, Dad!" "Thanks, fellows," he'd reply, he would hug them and kiss them good night. When Jack was late, I would sing and dance for them after prayer. I found that the music relaxed them. I'd improvise songs using their names and the things they did that day. I always had the radio on, so music played constantly. They loved "Rock-a-Bye Your Baby with a Dixie Melody." Sometimes I'd close with "Give My Regards to Broadway" and they'd hum along. Sometimes they'd fall asleep before I finished. A hug, a kiss, and a thank-you before they closed their eyes always put a smile on my face. On holidays Jack and I really hammed it up. It was fun watching their eyes glued to our entertainment. We had a captive audience, and it was easy to take advantage of their appreciation.

Every morning before Jack left for work, he'd go into their bedroom and call out, "Time to get up, everybody—*the sun is shining, the birds are singing, and the world is passing you by.*" For years, those words echoed in the boys' ears.

Our boys never heard disrespectful language in our household, but they sure knew how to argue amongst themselves over nothing. I'd listen until I couldn't stand it any longer, and then call out, "OK, boys, I'm going to call a conference, here and now, or would you rather stop that fighting? I'm tired of listening to the noise. It's your choice." Those were magic words, because the boys didn't like to give up any playtime and a conference could take up to three hours. They'd cut the noise and go on with something they all liked to do. Usually their little squabbles were settled quickly. Jack and I let the boys vent; it was a healthy way to communicate, and it strengthened our family. There were times when it was tiresome, but it was important to me to help them make things work. In the evening after all was settled I was more than ready, as Jack would say, "hit the sack."

We disciplined the boys both as individuals and, when the occasion warranted, as a group. One of the most effective ways I found to shape my sons' behavior was to show them how important it was to be useful and helpful to each other. Jack and I always tried to live our lives with intent, purpose, and with respect and consideration for each other. I would constantly thank them for the least little thing they did for each other, and they loved the recognition. It was easy for the boys to follow our example—most of the time.

When they squabbled, Terry would crawl up to them. There he was, his behind in the air, hands and feet on the ground, in the midst of a heated argument. He'd sit and glare back and forth at each of his brothers with two fingers in his mouth. The louder the argument, the faster he'd suck his fingers. That caught their attention; they'd shake their heads and quiet down. Terry would sit with one leg bent; if the boys tried to get away from him, he'd pump back and forth with the other heel to get where he wanted to go. It was a sight to watch and an effective way for him to get around. His favorite pastime was enjoying those two fingers in his mouth. He didn't have to talk, nor did he want to. And sometimes that was a blessing! As a baby and up until he was sixteen he was a complete joy to all of us. Sixteen I said, well more on that later.

Inglewood Home
Patrick two, Jackie Three, and Mom

United Air Lines Flight Returning from
San Francisco

Chapter 5

Moving to Fresno

*E*xactly six months to the day after we moved to Inglewood, Jack's company offered him the opportunity to move to Fresno, California, as manager of its new subsidiary. The business was expanding, and so was Jack's career. This was the opportunity he'd been wishing for, but he wasn't sure how I'd take the idea of leaving my family in Los Angeles. He did his best to paint a picture that would inspire me to want to move.

"It'll be easy," he assured me. "I'll help with all the packing and anything it takes to make this move easy for all of us." "Do we have a choice?" I asked. "Is this move necessary?" "If you feel it's too much for you," he began, but stopped when I nodded yes. "You mean it's all right?" "Yes honey; wherever you go, the boys and I want to be with you."

His face shone with enthusiasm. "I'd really like to try this," he said. "It's such a great opportunity. I've been with the company such a short time, and I was asked to go because other qualified men and their wives didn't want to leave the area. Are you sure it's OK with you? Naturally, I feel that your needs are our needs." When I told him I was sure, he asked when I could start packing. He planned to leave us behind until he could purchase a house in Fresno. "What a laugh!" I said. "Where are we going to get the money?" Jack said the company had offered to help us by working out an easy payment schedule. They would loan us the down payment for the house. In return we would rent our garage to the company converting it to an office for Jack. The rent for the garage would equal the mortgage payment. So there was no money out of our pocket. How could we go wrong? He was so excited and I said a silent prayer of thanks. He left for Fresno the next day to find our dream house. I packed our belongings and notified our relatives of our plans. The company obliged us with a car in order that I have everything ready when Jack returned for us.

As far as I was concerned there was only one problem. I hadn't told Jack I was already expecting our fourth baby, but I thought it best for him to concentrate on his new job. No need to worry him now! I felt pretty secure about managing until I could find a doctor in Fresno, but I must admit the memories of my previous difficult deliveries did frighten me. I told myself that, somehow, God would take care of me and things would work out.

The boys were exceptionally good travelers. When we arrived in Fresno, the house Jack found for us was still in escrow. He'd rented us a room with kitchen privileges in a motel right next to the Santa Fe Railroad track. Twice a day, the passing trains shook the ground, the motel, and everything in it. The vibration and noise was incredible. Who'd have believed this little motel would hold such fond memories! For it was there that Jackie, barely three and half years old, proved what a terrific big brother he was.

The first time a train roared by, Jackie knew why the floor was vibrating, but Patrick was so frightened that he froze and stood trembling. Jackie instantly ran to hug Patrick, assuring him that everything was OK and they were safe. Terry's eyes got as big as saucers as his little arms flew in the air, and I cuddled and soothed him until the train passed. It was quite an experience for us all.

In two weeks escrow closed and we wasted no time moving into our new home at 3462 Olive. This lovely two-bedroom, one-bath house had a large kitchen and eating area, a formal dining room, a large living room with a fireplace, and a small study. The house featured hardwood floors—which I became a slave to!—and plenty of storage space in all the rooms. The property was substantial, with a one-car garage, a carport with a laundry room behind it, and an enormous backyard. Two beautiful magnolia trees grew near the driveway. The boys were so happy that they did somersaults on the back lawn.

Our home was very plain and minimally furnished. With a house full of small boys who couldn't sit still for long, we felt that good, expensive furniture would meet with disaster. The only thing we bought new was our oblong chrome kitchen table with six chairs. It lasted for years. Shortly after we moved in we hung a 6'x4' green chalkboard on the wall behind the table. It was one of the most useful investments we made. The boys covered the lower portion with letters, numbers, words, and drawings. Without a doubt I would post the week's activities on it, and HAPPY BIRTHDAY always greeted celebrants at breakfast on their special day.

I often joked about having two bedrooms with all those boys. Their room contained bunk beds (which I hated), a twin bed, a crib, two chests of drawers, and a small toy chest. Little space remained for the boys to play; it was strictly a sleeping area.

We had plenty of room outside, though, and lots of trees. Two huge pine trees in the front yard overpowered the house. Eight rose trees lined the walk leading to the front porch, fruit trees lined both sides of the backyard, and there was a grape vine on the back fence. Close to the small patio we had another tree but it was only as tall as the top of the patio roof. In the far corner of the yard was a brick furnace where we burned our trash. In the opposite corner was a washroom as big as our garage with a workbench for Jack. Beyond that, six clotheslines were strung (there were no clothes dryers then). It was a residence designed for comfort and work.

The office needed to be moved from its present location to our garage. Jack wasted no time on the construction of the garage converting it to an office. The boys at the Fresno office graciously assisted Jack, after hours, helping him with this project. It was a great idea because this meant that Jack would spend much of his time close to home. I loved the idea. It wasn't long before Jack put me to work in that office counting the day's transactions with our new money counters. It was fun but time consuming for me.

Patrick, who was famous for climbing everything in sight, kept trying to climb the gigantic eucalyptus tree that grew in the middle of the back yard. One day he finally succeeded, but he couldn't get down. We had to call the fire department to rescue him. When the firemen arrived on the scene, one of them said, "This is a switch, we usually have to get cats out of this type of tree." Patrick was so frightened and he never climbed that tree again.

One afternoon I had an emergency and I needed to leave. I immediately took Terry and set him in his car-bed along with Jackie at my side. I told Pat to wait until I returned for him. As I entered the house for him I could see he was angry with me.

He quickly turned around and ran. I called for him to stop but he ignored me. I caught him in the living room and carried him quickly to the car. As I set him in the back seat he made funny faces at me. I did not realize that Jackie was holding on to the frame of the car door as I slammed it shut. He screamed with pain. Shocked I opened the door quickly to check his hand. He cried and cried as I tried to apologize. I'm so sorry honey as I cried with him. After a few seconds he said "It's OK now. It doesn't hurt too much." The door was shut just hard enough to crease his hand but did not break any bone. That night Jack checked his hand thoroughly. "His hand will be sore for a few days, honey but he is fine." It was a cheap lesson for the two of us.

One of Jack's friends, Paul Worsley, had an opportunity to purchase a burglar alarm business in Fresno shortly after we arrived. Jack was instrumental in helping him secure the business. The Worsley's were a complete joy to us. Paul was always there any time Jack needed him.

By this time I was eight months pregnant, I still had no idea to whom I should go for a checkup. Jack felt that it was time to do something. He discussed the situation with Paul, who consulted his wife, Alice. She found a doctor with an excellent reputation, in good standing in the community, and made an appointment for me right away.

The interview with Dr. Sharp went well, although he was astonished that I was eight months' pregnant and hadn't seen a doctor. He particularly showed concern when I described Terry's birth. He wrote to my previous doctor, inquiring about Terry's delivery. The answer implied that Terry's birth had been normal. It was hard to believe the report. There was very little time left to accomplish what my doctor ordered for me. Nutritionally I was deficient in vitamin K; I needed help.

Dr. Sharp was very strict, but I followed his instructions to the letter until it was time to head for the hospital. I was getting to the point where a little girl was less important than a normal birth. A little boy or a little girl was fine with me. Whatever; it is God's will.

Chapter 6

Our Fourth Son Arrives

*O*n Tuesday evening, May 9, 1950, I entered Saint Agnes Hospital in Fresno. The maternity ward was full of new mothers waiting to deliver. I was told that when my baby arrived they'd have a room for me. They put me on a gurney and placed me against a long white wall to wait for my time. A nurse assured me that I was going to be fine, but I wasn't too happy being in the hall with strangers walking back and forth. I just wanted to get this birth over with and go home.

At 10:45 P.M. our fourth son arrived. He weighed 8 pounds 2 ounces, stretched to 21 inches, and had fuzz for hair. Selecting names wasn't too difficult. I had hoped for Michelle Marie, and since Jack had picked the middle name of Gregory, we decided on Michael Gregory.

After my delivery I ended up back in the hall next to that wall! I motioned to the first nurse who passed by and asked to see my doctor. She said the doctor had gone home for the night. I was assured that my baby was fine, and that I'd see him soon. Shortly I was wheeled into a room with another lady who had just delivered her fourth baby. She was very friendly and stated that we had much in common. Her fourth child was a boy, too. "You're right," I said, "We do have something in common."

The nurse arrived with my baby and I felt history repeating itself. I checked him over thoroughly to see if everything was normal. Toes, fingers, eyes, ears, nose, and private parts were all in place. Then I thought, "Four boys! What in the world am I going to do with four of them? It's not fair."

In planning for my confinement, we got a babysitter for Jackie and Terry. Grandma Doris, who was living in Santa Barbara, wanted to keep Patrick with her until after Michael and I returned home. I was willing to let him go providing she would promise not to cut his beautiful long curly hair. Doris used to pick at me for one thing or another and one of her pet peeves was Patrick's beautiful hair. She told me she wouldn't cut it. "Promise," I said. So she pledged faithfully that she'd take only a brush or comb to his curls.

We packed Patrick's suitcase while I dried my tears. He hugged me and told me how much he loved me as Doris took him from my arms. I told Jack that he was too little to stay away from home. Even though we had agreed to let him go, I really didn't want him so far away from us. "Do you suppose that Patrick feels bad about our letting him go?" I asked. Jack assured me that it wouldn't dent his personality, that he'd have a great time, and he would be in the best of hands. I finally agreed, and Grandma Doris and Patrick headed for Santa Barbara.

On my third day in the hospital Jack brought me a card from Santa Barbara. I quickly tore open the envelope. It was a baby congratulations card from Grandma Doris. As I opened the card, something fell onto the bed. As I reached for it, I screamed. It was a bunch of Patrick's golden locks. "She broke her promise to me!" I wailed. "She cut Patrick's hair after she promised she'd only brush it." I was beside myself, and cried for days. Later she sent me a picture of him in his new haircut. He looked terrible with short hair. I felt betrayed.

Jack really felt bad about this. He didn't understand his mother's actions: unfortunately she felt that I wasn't good enough for her son, and she resented me. Cutting Pat's hair was a way of telling me she would do exactly as she pleased, and she was not pleased with our son's beautiful golden curls. I wanted Jack to go for Pat before I came home, but he felt that he was safe that I needed rest before he returned. So I agreed to wait, and turned my attention back to my new son. What little hair Michael had was straight and fuzzy. I knew I could never get a curl on top of *his* head!

During our stay in the hospital, the lady in my room, Gwen Simmons, became a close friend. She consoled me about Patrick, assuring me that his curls would come back in time. She was very pleasant, understanding, and sympathetic about my ongoing struggle with my mother-in-law. We remained good friends for many years. Our children were close in age and we celebrated birthdays and anniversaries together for over thirteen years. Her husband was an ear, nose, and throat specialist, and treated our children on several occasions.

In the late afternoon of May 15, 1950 Jack once again ushered our newborn son and me out of the hospital. As we drove home with Michael in my arms, I told my husband that I was exhausted by all these pregnancies. Perhaps later I might want to try for a girl, but now I needed rest. I'd had four sons within thirty-six months—that had to be a record! Jack was truly very understanding. When I asked him to accept the idea that there wouldn't be another baby next year, he agreed—and I gave a big sigh of relief.

When we arrived home the boys were waiting in the living room with open arms. Jackie insisted on holding Michael. He was old enough, so I showed him how to handle the baby and allowed him to cradle his baby brother for a while. He became such a great babysitter that I found myself taking advantage of him from time to time. Mrs. Syvertsen, a great German lady who lived across the street, lifted Michael from Jackie's arms and took him to his waiting bassinet. During the night I pulled the bassinet close to the bed where I could keep an eye on him. He was so bald I wondered just how long it would take before his peach fuzz would grow.

Late one evening, Grandma Doris called in response to Jack's appeal to bring Patrick home. She said they should be in Fresno early the next afternoon, and I told the boys that grandma was bringing Patrick home tomorrow. We were so excited that we planned a little party for him. Mrs. Syvertsen even baked a cake. When he arrived he was a little bashful, but eventually came over and hugged and kissed me. I picked him up and carried him to his baby brother. Patrick was so excited; all he wanted to do was kiss Michael's forehead and then hug and kiss me. It was such a joyous feeling—he was home and we were a family once again. I wanted to never let any of my children leave my side again. His haircut greatly changed his appearance, and it took time for me to adjust. As I ran my hand over his head, I noticed his hair wasn't as soft as it was before. It was course and stiff. I refrained from making an issue in front of Pat.

After a few days of getting around pretty well, I called the boys together. Even with Michael in my arms, I was able to capture their undivided attention; their eyes were glued to mine. As I watched them, I had to laugh within myself; I felt that they thought they were in trouble. I said, "The purpose of this gathering is to explain the importance of good behavior. What does that mean to each of you?" They giggled and said, "No noise." "Very good," I praised them. "I expect you to be considerate of both Michael and myself. You must think about our needs as well as yours. Michael and I need rest right now, so it's up to you boys. Do you understand what I'm saying?" They all nodded and smiled, and I continued.

"Mrs. Syvertsen will keep getting our lunches in the afternoon, and all of you need to help her. You know, take your plates off the table and help her wipe the dishes; whatever you can do to make her work easier, OK? I know she'll love that! Now, your toys can be a problem. It's very important that they be kept in the toy box when you're not playing with them. If I have the baby in my arms, and I step on one of the toys and fall, we both could be seriously hurt." "Oh, no!" they chorused "Well, it's important that you keep the floor clean at all times. I don't want Mrs. Syvertsen to have to pick up your toys for you. Also, please, no yelling; simply keep the noise down. I want you to keep close by in case I need some help with the baby." Then I walked over and sat on the couch, and each boy came over to kiss the baby and give me a hug. They were so dear. When I was stern with the boys, or laying down rules for them, I'd always try to remember that they're human beings—little guys, but mighty. I made it a practice to let them know just how much they were appreciated, and I would thank them regularly for little things. They'd show a certain amount of pride when I complimented them as a group, but individual praise worked like a charm.

Late one evening several months later, I heard a strange noise coming from the boys' bedroom next to ours. I jumped from my bed and ran into their room, only to find Michael standing in his crib, coughing hard and deep. I picked him up and rushed into my room to see him better. His face was turning blue. I turned him upside down and started to slap his back. I was so frightened that I did it frequently and hard. I'm not certain how long I banged

42

on him; I just know a big "poof" finally sounded, like whatever was in his throat came up and out. Michael then was pulling on my arm in order to assume a sitting position. And as I turned him upright I saw the color coming back into his cheeks. Whatever was in his throat was never found, but I really didn't care. His eyes were stern as he stared and cried. I kept him in bed with me, assuring him that he was OK until Jack arrived.

Jack finally came home and when he found him in bed with me, he was concerned. I explained what had happened and how frantic I was. He became excited but he checked Michael over just the same. He also checked Michael's crib; just to be sure there was nothing else he could put in his mouth.

The next day I held him constantly, concerned about how I'd banged on his back—surely he'd be sore—I wanted to keep him warm. I also told the boys what had happened. I explained the importance of keeping small items out of Michael's reach, and that we all had to be exceptionally careful with what he handled, because everything he picked up went into his mouth.

At nine months old, Michael still had not been baptized. Two of our dearest friends, the Cables were visiting one Sunday afternoon, and we asked them if they'd like to be Michael's godparents. They were delighted. They immediately took the reins, called the church, and made all the necessary arrangements for this beautiful celebration. The Cables bought a priceless white outfit and dressed him for the occasion. He looked so handsome in his new suit, but he wasn't happy with the sequence of events that day. With the pouring of the holy water over his head he made a real fuss, but his godparents managed to keep him calm. We thanked Father and left the church. Pictures were taken and dinner was served at a very special restaurant, all arranged by the godparents.

One Sunday morning after church, when Patrick was three years old, Jack wanted to go for a drive up the mountains. This was very unusual and I didn't want to turn him down; it was such a beautiful sunny day, so why not? "OK," I said, "let's go home first for a quick lunch to take with us." We did, and as we were leaving the house I asked Jackie and Patrick if they needed to go to the little boy's room. They both assured me they didn't. With Terry in a fresh diaper and baby Michael in his car bed, we all piled back in the car, excited about the outing.

As Jack drove around troubled curves one after the other at rather high elevations, Pat suddenly piped up, "I gotta go, Mommy." "What?" I replied loudly. "You said you didn't have to go before we left the house." "But I gotta go now," he said meekly. He was holding himself and jumping up and down in the back seat. When I told Dad he had better look for a place to stop, he said, "It's a steep embankment here; we have to be very careful." He parked close to the edge of the pavement to avoid endangering any passing vehicles, and then turned to Patrick and said, "I'll go around and get you, so wait for me, OK?" Pat had climbed over the seat and was standing at the passenger's door as I slowly opened it. Before I realized what was happening, Patrick pushed the door open and jumped out as Dad rounded the front of the car. I screamed as Pat disappeared down the embankment. When Pat hit the ground he knew he was in trouble; he immediately curled up, grabbed his ankles, and stuck his head between his knees. He rolled down that steep hill so fast he looked like a rubber ball. Nothing could stop him. I held my breath as I watched, frozen with fear.

Dad was so shocked and angry that he ran down that embankment in an almost lying-backward position, digging his heels in and not losing sight of Patrick for a second. When he reached the bottom Pat was just trying to stand up. Jack grabbed him by the shoulders of the heavy jacket he was wearing and shook him as angry words spilled out his mouth. He carried him by the jacket all the way up that hill with his temper flying. When they reached the top, Jack set him down and said, "Now go pee." Patrick sheepishly looked up and said, "I don't have to go." "What? You wanted to pee, so pee!" "I can't!" Pat cried as he stooped his shoulders, and Jack ordered him into the car. As he drove away Jack growled, "I can't believe what just happened. As a matter of fact, I've changed my mind. We're turning back, and we can have a picnic in our own backyard. At least it's safe there." Jackie was so disappointed, but he didn't complain.

Later that night, when all was quiet again, Dad saw the humor in the situation. He started laughing so hard he couldn't stop. "Can you imagine that kid doubling himself and rolling down that hill like a ball, that steep embankment? I can still see him, but I was so angry and worried at the same time. Too bad there wasn't a camera on him. When I reached the bottom and grabbed him as I did, he was so scared, and I'll bet he never does that again. Remember that, honey. That kid is going to take care of himself no matter what sort of situation he gets himself into. That was pretty clever. And he's just a little over three years old." Amazing!

"Yes, and after you were through with him, you scared the pee out of him! Poor Patrick, he sure learned a hard lesson today" We laughed for the longest time. After that incident Pat was good as gold. We didn't hear a peep out of him the rest of the week.

During this time I wanted to experiment with a garden. Jack suggested that the side of the garage would be a perfect place. The two of us cleaned the area and prepared it for planting. Later I announced to the boys that I was ready to plant the seeds in the garden. Pat says, "Can I help you Motho?" "Sure let's go." "You just take a pinch of seed with two fingers and plant them into this hole I have prepared." "OK." As he did I covered the seed. We planted carrots and radishes and watered the planted seeds carefully every day. As the plants broke ground Pat was so thrilled; he felt we had created a miracle.

Later one Sunday afternoon I announced to the gang I was going to wash my car. Again Pat says, "Can I help Motho?" "Sure, you can clean inside and I will wash outside. OK?" While wiping the windshield I noticed Pat in the front seat in deep thought. As I prepared the inside windows Pat says, "Motho, I would like to ask you a question!" "Ask me anything." "Looking me straight in the eye, he says, *Motho, where do babies come from?*" "That's a great question honey. Babies come from a seed." With a shocked expression on his face he said out loud *"You mean I came out of the ground?"* "Oh no honey, *you were so special.* You did not come out of the ground." It was such a relief to his mind; he hugged me and said, *"Oh, thank you Motho, thank you."* "The car is clean honey so it is time we get on to something else." "OK." He then in to the sand box where the boys were playing. That evening I told Dad about our conversation and he said, "Was he satisfied with your answer?" "I'm sure." "Three cheers for Mom!"

At a very early age, Michael's brothers taught him his ABC's and how to write his name, his address, his phone number, and the names of both parents. Much of this was done on that big green chalkboard on the kitchen wall. Michael loved to write and draw

45

on that board. He was quick to understand what the boys taught him, and was more than ready for kindergarten.

When Michael was six years old, someone gave him a Superman outfit for his birthday. Our young son thought he, too, could fly. He dressed up in his cape and told Jackie to watch, then hurried to the garage carport and appeared at the edge of the roof, arms spread out like wings, head straight up, Jackie instantly realized what he had in mind. At that very moment when Jackie shouted, Michael jumped—but instead of up, up, and away, he went straight down. He hit the ground on his belly with a thud and lay there on the grass. Jackie, shocked, ran to him. All Michael muttered was, "I want to go in the house and lie down." Jackie asked if he was all right. "I think so," was his reply, and Jackie helped him into the house.

Babysitter Jack was in the living room reading the paper, as usual. Michael walked over to talk to him. "Dad," he said, "I was Superman. I just jumped off the roof of the carport but I didn't fly; I fell to the ground instead." Jack replied, "Yes, I know, I know." As usual Jack's concentration on the paper blocked out what Michael was telling him. Michael went to his room to lie down. I was out shopping, and when I returned nothing was said to me about Michael's adventure. Jackie tended him constantly, saying nothing to Jack or me. Michael was shaken, but not injured. We were lucky. Michael never mentioned his adventure to anyone.

Never again did he dress up in his Superman outfit. I found it weeks later, stuffed under his bed. I folded it and replaced it in the toy box. Michael loved the Superman series on TV, but from that time on he ignored Superman. Since no mention of Michaels adventure reached my ears, I never became suspicious.

Chapter 7

Life in Fresno

Our life in Fresno from 1949 to 1960 afforded all of us many pleasures. We had our heartaches and headaches, but we were blessed with an enormous amount of love to go with it all. Not one of us ever interfered with Dad's busy schedule, nor did he ever interfere with our expensive activities. We always consulted him with our spending habits and he'd always remind us that there's always tomorrow. If something ever happened to him what would we do? He loved us and we loved him, and we had nothing to worry about as long as we did things together and within reason. Our attitude was that Dad would live forever.

Since the boys were all preschoolers, I was kept pretty busy. They were creative, and they kept me on my toes all the time. I was always correcting their manners or their English. For some reason they'd pronounce, "Mother" as "Motho." They knew it annoyed me, and they'd do it just to tease me. I corrected them endlessly, repeating myself until I finally gave up—figuring that, if all else failed, they'd call me "Mom."

The two older boys had individual responsibilities around the house. They knew they had to clean up their own messes and take care of their own toys and clothes. Terry was too young; he'd try to help, but his two fingers always got in the way. He'd have a ball just taking it all in, and that was good enough for me—one less problem to cope with!

Since Jack ran part of his business from home sometimes the phone would ring off the hook. At first those little guys would pick up the phone and then abruptly hang up on our customers. Jack was furious when his customers complained. This had to stop, so a conference was called. The boys were at play and I abruptly said

"In the den everybody." I proceeded to explain the phone problem. No one in this house is to answer the phone, no matter what. You boys are to act as though we do not have a phone. If it rings just leave it alone. If you pick up the phone you will have to stand in the corner; or my second offense you will have to kneel in the corner. That was their punishment from me; their father's was to utilize their own leather belts. In those days strict discipline was acceptable. With five boys we had no choice but to be strict, and I enforced the rules. (Dad would slap the table so hard with the leather belt the sound echoed through the house) "Next time it will not be the end of the table that catches the belt, he said. Do we understand each other?" It didn't take long for the boys to catch on. Only after they had demonstrated good phone manners (in about third grade) only then were they to answer the phone. Jackie was first to learn the script: "Nutter residence, Jackie Nutter speaking, may I help you?" Our friends—and customers— admired the boys for this.

Our sons were all good boys; they were full of life, but not wild. We gave them responsibilities and a certain amount of independence, and for the most part they handled themselves very well. They were all scrupulously honest. When confronted with their misdeeds, they would not lie, instead pleaded for time to solve their problems. "Mom, we do not want to lie to you, nor do we wish to tell you the truth right now. Please we need extra time." "Ok you got it."

On many occasions I had to report to Jack when some mischief was done and no one would admit to causing the problem. This happened much too often, and I felt it was time for Dad to get to the heart of the situation. He felt that if he wasn't there at the time, then he shouldn't be the one to punish them. "It's beyond me," I said. "Put your best foot forward and do something." He thought this out and decided on a unique solution. He called all the boys together in the backyard and told them that truth is of utmost importance in our household and he went on to say:

"Today there was a very serious problem here and Mom feels I should be the one to get things settled. I want you to remember that I don't like coming home and listening to this kind of junk. My days at the office are very busy and tiresome, and I want to come home and relax. I hope you all understand." All eyes were on him as he described the problem that day, although the boys glanced at each other often as he spoke.

"Now, in order to solve today's problem, I'm going to make it easy on all of you. Please come over here and stand directly in front of me. I'm going to ask each of you to stoop over and grab your ankles with your head completely down and between your knees. I will explain the problem and when I count to three, I want only the guilty boy to turn his head and look up at me. I promise I won't punish you. Do I make myself clear?" Each boy nodded yes. "OK," Dad said. "Everybody stoop over and grab your ankles. Keep your heads down and between your knees. On the count of three, remember, just the guilty person turn your head and look up at me. Ready? One … two … three."

All the boys' heads turned and looked up at the same time. Jack shook his head, put his hands over his face, and said to himself, "This isn't working." Then, to his sons, "OK, guys, let's talk. Let's sit here on the grass and have a nice long conversation."

I was in the kitchen getting dinner as I watched them. Jack preached to me how to discipline, yet his own strategy wasn't working. I was so glad I pushed him into this. Now he knows what I have been talking about. Of course, I also told him all the good things that happened. They really were very good boys; they simply had too many ideas running in their heads at that age.

Anthynette, our neighbor behind us, had a grandson, Lenny, who loved to come over and play with our boys when his parents visited his grandmother. On one occasion when he made his appearance, I had just called the boys in for a conference. Lenny threw his arms in the air and said, "Here I am, you lucky guys." With that, Michael told Lenny that I'd just called a conference, and he should come back later.

"How long, twenty minutes?" Lenny asked, and Michael replied, "No, Lenny, make it at least two hours." "Two hours?" he shouted. "OK then, but hurry. I'll be on the swings and I will wait for you." It sounded so funny I had to cover my face to keep from laughing. Lenny was Michael's age, but he loved all the boys and took an interest in anything they did.

That little Italian was always welcome. We treated him as if he was one of us and he loved it. He was happy to abide by our household rules. Anthynette (his grandmother) told me he was so

49

lonely, being an only child. His mother and father worked, and Lenny was alone most of the time. He was always happy when he was included in the boys' games. If he didn't understand, Jackie was good in showing and teaching. He was sharp and he caught on fast, and he never argued. He had quite a voice and as he glided high on the swing he'd sing his favorite songs to his heart's content. He loved "That's Amore" and his voice was loud and clear. His grandmother often had something for all the boys to snack on when Lenny was with her, and they'd all go across the alley for their treat of the day. We loved that little guy's music and we loved his grandmother.

Our Italian neighbors were extremely kind and thoughtful, and exceptionally patient with our boys. Almost every weekend their relatives gathered in their backyard, enjoying an endless array of food and conversing for hours. The Italian language fascinated our boys and they would listen with deep interest.

Our neighbor's children were grown with the exception of the youngest daughter, Irene, who was fifteen. When Terry was about five years old he'd sing all the time. The song he liked best was "Good Night Irene." He'd sing as loud as he could when Irene was in sight, hoping she might hear him. When I asked him why he sang at that particular time, his comment was, "Mom, she's so beautiful." I asked, "Are you teasing her, or do you think she likes to hear you sing?" "No," he said, then tipped his head and added, "I'm not sure, but I think I love her." "Really?" "Yes," with another pause, "I think someday I might marry her." "What do you think Irene would say if she knew how you felt?" "I'm not sure," he replied and then ran off to play with his brothers.

Chapter 8

Boys and Other Small Animals

*A*nimal's had to be a part of our family life. One day when Terry was in the first grade at Sacred Heart School, he was walking home when a lady with a big dog drove by in a Cadillac. She stopped and asked Terry if he'd like to have a free dog. "A free dog?" Terry asked. "Yes," she replied, then handed him the leash of the dog in the car and told him the dog's name. She told him to tell his mother when he got home to tie the dog up for four days, and he'd have a beautiful dog for as long as he wanted him. Terry smiled and thanked her, then helped the dog out of the car. As that dog hit the ground he started to run, and Terry hung onto the leash for dear life.

I happened to walk out the front door just as he and the dog went flying by. I was so shocked that all I could do was yell, "Terry, let go of that dog!" But the leash was around Terry's wrist and he couldn't let go. I ran after him screaming, "Let go!" and by the time I caught up he'd managed to stop the dog. He told me the story as he tried to catch his breath. "Where is this lady, and where is the car now?" I demanded furiously. He huffed and puffed, "I don't know, she left." I couldn't believe a grown woman would give such an animal to a first-grader without a parent's consent, and then, worse, watch what was happening and do nothing about it. But Terry was already pleading, "Can we keep him? Please, Mom?"

What was I to do? After all he'd been through I talked to Dad, and we agreed to keep him. We tied the dog to the back clothesline, and he seemed to settle down. I fed him and kept a bowl of fresh water for him. After four days I released the dog's chain, and

I kept a watch on him from the kitchen window. We had a six-foot fence with a gate we kept locked at all times, and that dog would sit for the longest time and just stare at the gate. He paid absolutely no attention to the boys or his food or water.

One afternoon the dog bolted; he cleared the gate with ease and kept going. We never saw him again. Worried about Terry's reaction, I prepared to console him when he came home from school. After I'd explained what had happened, Terry thought for a minute and said, "I guess that dog just didn't love us," and went to his room. He wasn't the least bit broken-hearted. What a lesson I learned that day!

Not long after this, he called out to me as he walked into the backyard. When I responded, he said, "Look, Mom, this little guy followed me all the way home!" It was a beautiful puppy, barely six weeks and hardly able to stand on all fours. I said, "Is that right? Well, let me tell you, son, you're going to have to turn right around and let that little guy follow you back where you got him." "Oh, he's so tired, and I don't think he can do it." So I scooped him up and told Terry to get into the car because we were taking this little guy back. Terry didn't feel the least bit bad, nor did he plead with me to keep him this time. When we returned home Terry said, "That Poor Baby".

In 1953 Jack brought a baby lamb home as a pet for the boys. The boys would take turns bottle-feeding the lamb three times a day. Jack built a special pen for him and the boys decided to call him Lambkin, but sometimes they called him Baby. When Lambkin got too big and it was time for lamb chops, we all decided to take him to a ranch where he could run and play with other animals.

We had two Hamsters and quickly named them Pat and Mike. They liked to sit on our shoulders and nuzzled down our necks, and we all enjoyed their affectionate attention. We thought we had two boys, but discovered one morning that one had produced eight tiny babies. They were precious and the pet store loved us, but after three quick multiple deliveries I decided to call it quits and talked the boys into another pet. So Squeaky, a white rat, entered into our household—God help me.

Tropical fish were Michael's specialty. He attended their every need; he was good about keeping the tank clean, and gave them special food on a regular basis. We all enjoyed his aquarium, and I was glad to have such quiet pets!

Michael also brought baby chicks home. As I watched him walking in the circle driveway with those chick along side of him I couldn't believe my eyes. Dad had to build a special pen for all of them. As if that wasn't enough, he was lucky enough to bring home a pair of geese on a leash, given to him by one of the neighbors. Another corral had to be built. Soon mama was sitting on a couple of eggs, and papa allowed nobody near her. He became very nasty, and made horrible noises when anyone came near there home base. Papa goose was the best "watchdog" we ever had! Unfortunately the neighbor's dog killed mamma goose before the eggs were hatched and who hatched them, big brother Jack with special lighting.

The third time—would you believe it?—A dog that followed Terry home was different. She was an adorable cocker spaniel—dachshund mix with black and white markings. Surely whoever lost her would want her back. I advertised in the newspaper and on the radio, but got no response. We decided to keep her, and called her Lady. Her name really fit: she'd been well trained and she was gentle. She ruled the roost in the house for a long time.

She was never allowed to jump on guests, our furniture, or on beds, or to sleep with any of the boys. She'd stay with the boys as they said their prayers at night and played as much as was allowed, but when it was time to go to sleep, we'd say, "OK, Lady, time to hit the sack." Each boy would hug her and say goodnight, and off she'd go to her own special bed. She never made a fuss, but she made sure everyone was awake first thing in the morning.

One afternoon, I didn't notice that Lady had jumped into the car before I drove off. When I reached my destination, I thought I felt her breath on the back of my neck. As I turned around I saw her standing up behind me, looking out the window and panting away. I turned too look at her, saying, "Lady, what in the world are you doing here? You're a bad girl." I was really annoyed. It was summer, and because she was in the car I had to leave the car window down while I shopped. I told her that I'd be back shortly and to say put. Normally, those words were enough for her to be obedient. I did my shopping and when I came out, Lady was gone. I was so upset; I called her name and went all over looking for her. After an hour of searching I panicked. She had never strayed before and she never went anyplace without one of us. Surely she was close by, but where?

I was exhausted with worry, afraid that she'd be killed in traffic, or that someone might pick her up and take her home. When I got home I called Jack told him what had happened. He said, "Lady's a very smart dog and I don't believe she'd go with anyone. Why don't you call the radio station? Have them announce Lady's name every half hour, and offer a reward to whoever finds or sees her." I immediately placed the call.

The station made the announcement every half hour for one full day. The boys were getting worried since she'd been gone so long. I assured them we'd find her. Toward evening of the second day, a lady called to say she'd seen Lady hiding in a shopping center. She told me that when Lady's name was called she wouldn't let anyone near her, but ran away. Perhaps, she said, if Lady heard my voice she'd come to me. It was so late and so dark that I felt uncomfortable going out, but if it was really Lady out there all by herself, I had to go.

When the call came the boys were in their pajamas and ready for bed. I didn't tell them about the call; I didn't want to get their hopes up if I couldn't find her. I drove to the shopping center as directed and parked under a streetlight. I called out to her several times before I saw something moving in the distance. I stood under the light and kept calling her name. It was our Lady, all right; she took off at a dead run, and when she leaped at me I caught her in mid-flight. She wouldn't stop licking me, and I was as happy to see her, as she was to see me. Her coat felt sticky and dirty, but I didn't care as I held her close. We drove to the house to see who'd reported her, whom I thanked as I handed over the promised reward.

Lady snuggled in my lap all the way home, licking her paws. They were dry and rough from the hot sidewalk. The minute we got home she made a beeline for the boys' room. She jumped on all the beds and licked each boy several times until we calmed her down. The minute that Jack, arrived home that evening it was the same thing all over. I treated her paws with some cream, and as I did she licked my hands. That night and only that night was she permitted to sleep in the boys' room? The next morning I bathed her, usually she hated that, but this time she loved the attention. She was so beautiful and so happy. For days afterward, she'd lie on the living room floor with her chin on her paws, watching the boys' every move. We could almost read her mind. We all adored that little dog so much. There were many other dogs after Lady that Terry brought home, but none remained with us. Lady wouldn't allow it. She was part of the family and she wasn't leaving and no body was going to take her place.

The last animal Terry brought home was a monkey, and I had to buy a cage. That monkey turned out to be mean. Every time Terry attended him with food and water, the monkey would bite him. Terry himself decided to look for the original owner; he was tired of all the bites, and it didn't appear that the monkey would ever cooperate—much less be affectionate.

Terry spread the word among his friends that he'd found a monkey, and let them know if anybody knew its owner to contact us. One afternoon a young boy came to our door and told us he was the owner of Fred, his missing monkey. When Terry invited him in, the boy took one look at the monkey and said, "Yes, that's Fred all right." Terry asked, "Do you have a cage for Fred?" "Well, not really." "Well, Fred really needs a cage, so be my guest and take his new cage with you." "Are you sure?" "Yes" (as I nodded my approval). "Oh, thank you!" We waved goodbye to Fred—and were happy never to see him again.

It was a long time before another animal came to us through the efforts of our number-three son. Terry felt that it was time for the animal kingdom to look after itself. What a relief for me!

Chapter 9

Pregnant Football and Art Classes

*O*n many occasions people told me how lucky I am to have such fine sons. Of course, I agree! But I believe raising children is more than a mere work of love and duty. Truly, it's a profession, as important as any job that earns a paycheck. For me, the profession of being a mother proved challenging and interesting. It certainly demanded my best. I don't believe luck is the main factor in raising fine children. Our family's commitment to each other, our love and compassion, meant that, in a very real way, we made our own luck as we went along.

After breakfast one morning when I was in bloom with our fifth child, I talked the boys into playing in the backyard. Usually they'd empty their toy box and spread the clutter across their room, so I suggested different outdoor games. They thought it was a good idea, so they picked out some toys they wanted and headed outside.

It wasn't long before tempers started to fly. They were arguing about nothing, but it was fierce. I finally told them if they didn't calm down they'd have to sit in corners until they could behave. That was my best form of punishment and the best way to keep them calm and quiet around the house, but it bored them to death and they hated it. When I told them to figure out something they could play and enjoy together, they put their heads together—and chose football.

Jackie called to me, "It's easy for you to tell us to play something else. But how can we play football with just the four of us? We don't have enough players."

I yelled back, "You should be so lucky! Some kids only have one brother, or just themselves. Stop looking for excuses.

Otherwise, come in the house and two of you play checkers, and the other two play chess. That's an easy remedy, how about it?" Jackie said, "No, we want to play football, but we really need another player. Mom, please! Come out and join us."

I was close to seven months pregnant and as big as a house. And I'm only five feet tall. I tried to reason with them. "Listen, fellows, I cannot play with you. Football requires a lot of running and look at me. Not only can I not run, but also it would be too hard on my heart. It is impossible and much too difficult for me, so please figure out something else." Jackie thought for a minute, and then explained his idea to me.

"Mom, Mike and I want you on our side. I'm going to be the quarterback, so I'll pass the ball to you and you can run for an easy touchdown. I'll keep Pat and Terry away from you. As it is, Terry is so slow he can't do anything." He added that Terry wasn't too sure about the rules of the game anyway. "It's going to be a cinch. Then presto, Mom! Touchdown and we win. OK, please?" This is 1952 and Jackie is only six years old, but very knowledgeable in football rules.

I thought for a minute and then repeated, "Jackie, I simply cannot run." He said, "You don't have to run. Just walk fast." I was so skeptical, but foolishly I agreed. "Okay ... but you have to take good care of me." "No worry, Mom, no worry."

As I walked into the backyard, he explained that the west side was the goal post and it was there I had to carry the ball. We started our huddle supposedly on the fifty-yard line. I called time out immediately. "Why do we have to be on the fifty-yard line? Why can't we start on the one-yard line? Then I'm sure I can make a touchdown." "Mom, I wouldn't be able to control Pat, he'd slaughter you immediately." "You know, Jackie, I've see you play with Dad, and he has a difficult time controlling Pat. He's so quick and so fast, and so slippery; now tell me what makes you think you can control him?" "Mom, believe me, I can. So let's get started."

We took our places, and then Jackie did the count down and threw me the ball. I caught it, tucked it under my arm and took off with what I thought was lightning speed. Little did I realize the energy it would take to walk fast, let alone run! Both Jackie and Michael screamed several times, "Go, Mom, go!" I thought I was going to make it, but then I looked back and saw Patrick break away from Jackie, running with all his might after me. Jackie, in hot pursuit, missed him every step of the way. Pat charged, flung himself into the air, and came down with his arms wrapped around my legs. My stomach hit the ground so hard it almost knocked the wind out of me; I must have bounced back up like a rubber ball. I was stunned and mad at the boys, and they knew it.

When I could roll into a sitting position I saw those boys all together laughing so hard at the sight of poor me trying to catch my breath and trying to get up on my feet. Not one of them realized the danger I was in. To hit the ground on your stomach and bounce had to be funny. Michael was laughing just as hard as the other boys, but he came over and said, "I don't think you should play anymore, Mom. Jack, we can't let Mom play anymore." Michael tried to help me up, but he was too little. I rolled over on my knees in order to get up.

Jackie was so weak from laughing so he could hardly walk, let alone pick me up. When I was finally able to catch my breath, I said, "What did you say about keeping Pat away from me? What happened to those legs of yours?" Holding his stomach, Jackie finally managed, "I'm so sorry, Mom, but Pat just kept slipping away from me." Patrick said, "Motho, you were on Jack's team, and I couldn't let you make that touchdown." "Thanks a lot," I said, as I tried to regain my composure. "Well, number-two son, you're too fast for me, and so your team wins. Right now I want to go in the house and rest." Pat was only five years, but he was lightning in himself.

The boys helped me to the couch, not fully aware of the game's consequences to me. I parked myself for the rest of the morning, and prayed. When it came time to eat I called the breed in and told them I wasn't able to fix lunch. They said they'd take care of it. When they brought my lunch they told me I'd looked so funny with Pat's arms around my legs as I fell, and I'd bounced so hard that I looked like a rubber ball. I agreed that it must've looked funny, but there'd be no more football for me. Jackie said, "I'm really sorry, Mom. I'll never let you try that again."

That evening when Jack came home the boys told him about our morning incident. He was so mad at me, and couldn't believe that I'd do such a thing. "You know how fast Patrick is, and you boys have absolutely no business asking Mom to play football with you. She can't play those types of games. Jackie, you're old enough to know better. You boys should be taking care of Mother, not leading her into danger." I agreed that I shouldn't have done it, but said I was OK now and I'd never do anything like that again. Dad said, "You should've called me right away and I would've taken you to the doctor." I assured him that there was nothing to worry about.

Jack prepared dinner for us, and after we'd finished the boys cleaned up the kitchen in complete silence. After a couple of hours of TV they showered and readied themselves for bed. I didn't have to ask them to do anything; they knew what to do and they did it. What a peaceful evening it was!

That night as the boys knelt beside their beds for prayer, they asked God to forgive them for being so rough on their Mom that day. After Jack tucked them in I kissed each one goodnight. I thanked them for doing the dishes after dinner and for being so obedient the whole evening. It was such a pleasure and I wanted them to know it.

As Dad and I watched TV I noticed him watching me out of the corner of his eye. I was nestled in his arms, and I asked him if he was OK. He said, "It's not I to be concerned about. Are you sure *you're* OK? Perhaps I should take you to see the doctor tomorrow and you can tell him what happened today." I told him I felt fine, but if I didn't by morning I would call the doctor myself.

At this time our oldest son was only six, and the youngest was three; they were babies themselves. Still, they had the presence of mind to prepare our lunch and clean up afterwards, do the dishes in the evening, and get themselves ready for bed—without a single word of complaint from any of them. Thinking about it now really makes me proud. They were so young.

Grandma Doris lived with us off and on in Fresno, and made life very difficult. She was clever enough never to pick on me in front of the boys, but she did not hesitate one little bit to degrade me in Jack's eyes. She criticized my clothes, cooking, housekeeping, driving, child-rearing methods, and especially my careless extravagance with Jack's money (*his*, not ours, in her mind). This upset Jack deeply. He tried to convince her that she was wrong until he was worn out. It was a terrible situation. Never did we want the little boys to know of her resentment, because they loved their grandmother and we wanted to keep it that way. When Doris was in a rare good mood it was great to be around her, but when she was unhappy she made Jack and I miserable. He was her number two Son. He was so happy and that alone should have pleased her.

I decided to do something about Doris, so I enrolled her in an art class. Reluctantly, she agreed to go, so I drove her there. The class really impressed her. I purchased a variety of paints, brushes, and other items to get her started. (The only time she didn't complain about my lavish spending!) It was one of the best investments I ever made; she discovered she loved to paint, and continued to take classes. From then on she was too busy creating paintings rather than pick fights with me, and she refrained from keeping Jack up with her complaints.

She never let me forget that I wasn't good enough for her son, but nevertheless I won her over to a degree. Once she admitted that the only good thing about me was that I kept the boys clean, fed and the house clean. When I thanked her, she sniffed, "Well, I suppose you could consider that as a compliment." I hated her attitude, but I made it a point to get along. After all she was Jack's Mom.

Chapter 10

Our Fifth and Final Son

*O*n October 23, 1952, Jack drove me to Fresno Community Hospital. This time he remained very calm. He talked all the way there, professing his love for me and thanking me for agreeing to have this baby. When we arrived at around 10 P.M. with my labor off and on, the doctor and staff were already in the delivery room. Our other sons were born on Tuesdays, but this one decided to enter our family on a Thursday.

For no apparent reason, my labor stopped. My body was at a standstill; I had absolutely no pain. After all the prep work I was positioned on the delivery table like a mummy. As the minutes ticked by, both my doctor and anesthesiologist started to worry. The doctor asked if I wanted a spinal. After he explained what was involved, I agreed. There was no time to loose.

The anesthesiologist quickly prepared me while my doctor held me in a sitting position with my legs dangling to the floor. After the shot in my spine I felt absolutely nothing, nor could I do anything. Both doctors did the pushing and pulling. After a few minutes our fifth son weighed in at a strapping 9 pounds 4 ounces, 21 inches long. The doctor laid Dennis on my stomach. Both doctors were working fast because the afterbirth wasn't moving. I stayed awake during all this hustle and bustle, entirely at ease. I felt they knew what they were doing, and I was busy admiring my son.

I cuddled Dennis as he squirmed, his eyes searching and blinking, trying his level best to look around. He was so chubby that his little wrists and ankles were hidden in fatty tissue. He was perfectly normal and before I knew it the nurse took him from me. The doctors had finished their work and I was then wheeled to my room with a promise from the nurse that she'd bring Dennis back once he was clean.

As usual I spent my days in the hospital flat on my back; I wasn't allowed to sit. The doctor had ordered daily heavy doses of penicillin to ward off any infection that he feared because of the problem after Dennis was born. On the fourth day my mouth, face, hands, and arms felt like one big blister. I could hardly swallow and had trouble breathing. When the nurse came with another shot, I begged her to forget it. "Look at me!" I said, and when she checked me over she called the doctor. Immediately the shots were stopped and gradually my body returned to normal, but it took more than six months. I've been allergic to penicillin ever since.

My departure from the hospital was no different than previous. I was concerned about my sons, patiently waiting to see the baby before bedtime. Mrs. Syvertsen, bless her, had kept all four boys this time. Leaving the hospital the nurses again chorused, "See you next year!" No thanks, I thought. Five boys, a dog, a cat, and a busy husband were all I could possibly handle right now.

When we arrived home Jack helped the two of us out of the car and up the steps. As he opened the door I heard voices in the bathroom down the hall. Mrs. Syvertsen saw us and quickly opened the bathroom door. The boys were getting ready to vacate the tub when Mom and Dennis appeared. I've often wished that Jack had taken a picture that night. It would've been priceless, with all the boys in their birthday suits.

All eyes were upon us as their little hands reached up. I fell to my knees with Dennis in my arms and hugged each one of them. I said, "Look what I have here," as I pulled back the shawl from Dennis's face so they all could see their little brother. Their eyes glistened and smiles brightened their faces as they oohed and aahed. Each wanted to caress the baby. "He's so beautiful!" "His eyes are closed." "Can we kiss him?" "Of course," I said, "but kiss him on his forehead, let's not wake him. You may also kiss his little cheeks, but very gently." As each one kissed him they cupped his cheeks adoringly in their hands.

As we all stood and admired our little guy, I asked them if they thought they could help me with him, saying, "He represents a great deal of work." Jackie replied, "You have nothing to worry about, Mom, because we're going to help you care for this little brother of ours." I kissed boys and told them I needed to rest now. I was exhausted, and Dennis was sound asleep as Jack laid him in the bassinet.

As I rested, troubling thoughts crept into my mind. As good as the boys are and as patient as Jack is, can I still handle all these boys? Before Dennis arrived I'd worried about my ability to manage all the trials and tribulations of the future. It was rather late to be thinking this way, but at this point, I realized I had reached my limit. I needed to have a long talk with Jack. He simply had to accept some of this responsibility. Keeping me barefoot and pregnant wasn't going to work any longer. There would be no more babies in our household, at least not from me. I was destined for boys and as long as I had five, I wanted to sit back and enjoy them.

Jack finally agreed and felt that he was parent-qualified by now; therefore, it was time for him to allow me the opportunity to rest from any more pregnancies. We now can lead a normal and tranquil life. Amen.

Chapter 11

Growing Pains

*L*ong before Jackie entered kindergarten, he knew his ABC's and how to write his name, address, and telephone number. We taught him about his grandparents, and he knew what his Dad did for a living. There were no secrets in our household, but I found that I needed to be ever so careful of my words—everything that happened at home was talked about at school. Jack and I were careful about the words we used in front of our boys. What we didn't want them to hear, we did in private, behind closed doors.

In September 1952 Jackie started kindergarten at Chester Rowell. His first day was terrible. When we arrived I introduced him to his teacher and then asked him to sit with the other children. I explained that he was going to play with them and have lots of fun, and that he'd learn much more than I'd taught him at home. He was nervous and wouldn't let go of my hand. I gently pulled away, but he wouldn't take his eyes off me. Finally we were able to slip out the door. We made for the car, which was parked in front of the classroom. The moment Jackie missed me he ran to the window and looked out at us, crying and screaming "Mommy!" so hard that I wanted to go back. Jack said. "He'll be OK" as we drove back home. "His teacher will take care of him. I know how bad you feel honey, given time and he will be alright. If you run back to him now, then he's learned nothing." I blurted out, "I can't help it," as I tried to control my tears.

Chester Rowell was only four long blocks from our house, and Jack insisted that Jackie (and later, all the boys) walk to and from school. After his second day, Jackie made the daily round trip alone. He knew he wasn't to speak with anyone on the street, and was never to go play with a friend before coming home first.

He understood the rules and was obedient, until one day when he saw a lady whose young son had a fistful of candy. This attracted Jackie, and he stopped and stared. The mother told her baby to give Jackie a piece of his candy. When he didn't, she took a piece from him and gave it to Jackie.

That baby was so upset that he screamed as the tears flowed down his cheeks. Jackie was so concerned that he returned to the baby and handed the candy back. He started to walk away again, but the baby reached out his fist, offering a small bag of candy. Jackie, elated, picked out five pieces and thanked the baby. He then told the lady he had four brothers at home to share with, and that I was waiting for him. She wrote down her telephone number and told Jackie to give it to me if I had any questions.

By this time I was getting pretty concerned, and when I heard the big gate open, I greeted him at the kitchen door. Jackie ran up the stairs and pulled the candy from his pockets, and as the boys gathered around I questioned him. He told me what had happened and how he'd handled the situation. I marveled over his explanation and his behavior. He gave me the lady's note, and when I called her that evening she explained the details. She was most complimentary about Jackie's behavior, and I thanked her for her kindness.

I told Jackie I was proud of him, and that his training at home had taught him how to govern himself in a situation such as this, but nevertheless I didn't want this to happen again. If he wanted something, no matter what it was, he was to come to me; if I felt it was OK for him to have it I would get it for him. He said that he just wanted to bring something home to the boys. I thanked him for his thoughtfulness, and his brothers hugged him and thanked him too.

The morning after Dennis and I came home from the hospital Jackie didn't want to go to school. He was excited about his new brother and wanted to help me care for him. Jack convinced him that school was a necessity; and besides, he said, who would announce our new arrival to his class? He promised to have Dennis' picture taken so that Jackie could show it to his classmates. Without hesitation Jackie agreed and sat down to breakfast with the other boys. He did his early morning chores and then he and Dad were on their way to school.

When Jackie returned home that afternoon, he told us he'd discovered something really special. His classmates' moms were expecting babies too. He'd explained to the class what a happy time it is when a new baby enters the house and how excited everyone gets. He was quite a spokesman for his family.

On many occasions the four boys would jump into bed with me in the morning while we cuddled Dennis in the middle of the bed to admire him. The boys were amazed the day he discovered his hands and feet. Dennis kept his brothers busy just watching him reach out to them and the world around him.

Our number-one son was always doing something for his little brothers. It's not that they didn't do for him, but his constant thought was to help them or give them something whenever he could—not only material things, but sound advice as well. This continued throughout his life. His thoughtfulness and consideration have always been a joy to all of us.

One afternoon Jackie told me his hand hurt constantly. I checked it and could see nothing. "Ok, Jackie it is time to see the doctor." I called for an afternoon appointment. The doctor could see his hand was sensitive. He said, "Mrs. Nutter you need to soak his hand in warm water all evening and return in the morning." "You understand Jackie." "Yes." First, I set him by the television with a large bowl and warm water. I kept adding water, but it was hopeless. Secondly, before bedtime I set a wet warm washcloth in and around his hand and placed his hand in a plastic bag. Third, I wrapped his hand around a large towel along with a heating pad pinned around the towel. I told him it was going to be difficult to sleep, but it was necessary. Early the next morning Jackie called to me. *"Mom, I cannot feel my hand anymore."* Immediately I removed everything and we witnessed such an infection in the palm of his hand. "Hurry honey get dressed, we need to get to the doctor's office." The doctor took one look at his hand and said, *"This is the best soaked hand I have ever seen in my entire life."* With a sterile knife he pierced the center of the infection. Cleaned it, wrapped it and told me to retire Jackie for a couple of days. "Keep his hand clean and bandaged and the healing process will take effect." Jackie was obedient and in a few days his hand was back to normal. Amen.

The following year Patrick entered Chester Rowell. He was somewhat more aggressive in school than Jackie; it got him into trouble from time to time, but nothing serious. Surprisingly enough, he received plenty of coaching from Jackie about the in and outs of kindergarten. His first day of school was a cinch; no crying for him or me! Jackie had told him which toys were the most fun, and Pat made a beeline for them at playtime. He was already learning to share at home, but it was different at school. It was a hard lesson for him, but his teacher was patient and he listened and learned. If his classmates beat him to the good toys, he managed to wait until they tired of them. His teacher told me later that Pat was a little gentleman, very courteous to his classmates.

Like Jackie, Patrick soon learned to walk home from school and did it with pride. He'd ring the front doorbell when he got home and we'd make a big deal of his arrival. Each boy would hug him and tell him he was missed, and then he'd enthrall them with stories of the day's adventures. He brought everything he made home to his brothers, and he kept his school things in a special folder. At night after his bath he not only put his shoes under his bed very neatly, he also lined up every pair of his brothers' shoes under their bed. He always gathered everyone's soiled clothes and put them into the hamper. It was obvious that he loved neatness, and he loved it when his brothers thanked him for his efforts.

Jackie and Pat slept in bunk beds, and Patrick, being a still, quiet sleeper, rated the top bunk. One night he had a bad dream and moved around so much that he fell out. He hit the chest of drawers on his way down and dragged his bottom lip against it. That resulted in a pulled muscle and a large lump just above his chin. It was several years before that lump smoothed out.

The boys made their first Holy Communion and their Confirmation. Those were special days. I loved watching my sons, who looked so pure and innocent, as the Bishop touched each little head and asked the Lord to protect them with heavenly grace. All the boys except Dennis were altar boys. They sang in the choir on Sundays and on special holidays. Their teacher was especially proud of them. Their voices were loud and clear and they all looked especially neat in their white smocks as they sang. Monsignor once approached the boys and told them that at least one of them should consider becoming a priest. The boys looked at each other, shook their heads, and said, "Well, maybe someday, Monsignor, maybe someday."

Every Sunday the boys and I went to communion together. One Saturday in 1953 Jack drove our oldest son to confession, and it bothered Jackie that his dad took him, but did nothing himself. On the way home he asked his father if he was afraid of the confessional. Dad replied that wasn't the case, that he simply didn't share our religious beliefs. Jackie did not understand. When they came home from church Jack told me about their conversation in the car. I knew that my husband was a spiritual man, and that going to church with us every Sunday wasn't meaningful enough for him. I asked what he was going to do about it, and he replied, "I guess there's a simple answer."

Jack asked our pastor about converting to Catholicism. Our pastor named classes he should take in order to make his First Communion. Despite Grandma Doris' violent objections, Jack completed the classes, and the day he made his first Holy Communion was such a thrill for all of us. Jackie stood in for his father as he took his vows, and we all watched with shining eyes, full hearts, and heads held high. All of us remember dearly the beautiful scene in front of the altar that Sunday afternoon. Dad too was proud of himself.

The next Sunday was filled with pride as we all walked up to the communion altar together. Jack was so proud of himself that he took all of us out for breakfast afterwards. He was an exceptional husband and father—thoughtful, considerate, kind, handsome and intelligent. I always told him that he looked as if he stepped off the cover of a magazine when he left for work in the morning. He was the ringmaster of our family and we loved and respected his needs.

Jack's mother, Doris, was beside herself after her son's conversion. It then became very difficult to please her. After several months of complaints it became such a strain I therefore, decided something had to be done. One morning as Jack was leaving for work, I cornered him by his car. I told him that I did not want to come between him and his mother; therefore, I am hoping to find an apartment for the boys and myself. Hopefully by this weekend all six of us will be gone. He was so shocked he pulled me close to him and held me in his arms for a few seconds. "Please honey;

you don't know what you're saying. I know grandma has been difficult for both of us but give me a couple of weeks and surely I can find something for her." I questioned him how and what. I said, "She constantly complains that she has no money. Honey I simply cannot continue to give her money when she complains." Jack then realized that she could no longer live under our roof. He promised he'd work something out. I knew I could not leave nor did I want to. Within a few weeks, Jack had found his mother a nice little house about fifteen minutes from ours. Three cheers for Dad! She loved her little residence and weekends gave us a chance to visit her with little gifts for her new home. That made the boys happy and our household was back to normal again.

One weekend Terry decided he wanted to go visit Grandma. It was so hot outside we decided to stay home where it was cool. Dad said "OK guys?" All agreed. After a couple of hours I realized that Terry was missing. The temperature outside was 103 degrees in the shade and to go outside was a real effort. Finally I could stand it no longer so I ventured to the patio and called out to Terry. As I did, two Fresno police were walking in the drive with Terry sitting on the officers' shoulders. My mouth flew open as the officer explained they found Terry on Shields and Blackstone jumping up and down on the hot sidewalk. Terry explained his dilemma to them and they told him they needed to take him home. Terry was only too happy to direct them to the house. As the officer set Terry down he said, "I wanted to go see grandma." I thanked these uniformed men as Terry ran in the house and explained to dad about his trip. Dad did not believe him until I explained what just happened outside. Jack shook his head in disbelief with our young son. "Well, tell me son, did you learn something today." "Yah dad, that sidewalk was so hot; I'm not going to do that again." We were lucky it was the Fresno Police who spotted him.

At about age five and before he entered kindergarten, Patrick decided to leave home. He took his suitcase out of the closet and packed it. He came into the kitchen where I was preparing lunch and told me he wanted to leave home. I wasn't sure what he meant, so I asked him where he wanted to go. "I'm not sure," he replied. "OK," I said. "Let's sit right here and talk about it." When I asked if he was unhappy, he replied, "I don't think so." I asked if he was angry with his dad, his brothers or me. "No." "Well then, I don't understand."

"I just want to go away," he replied. "Would you like me to drive you?" I asked. "No." "Well, you can't leave without some food and clothes," I remarked, as casually as I could. "Would you like me to pack you a lunch?" "No, I have money." "Well, how about some extra clothes? You can't leave with just those clothes you have on." "I packed my suitcase already." "Well, OK, if that's what you really want." He nodded. All this time he'd been looking down at the floor; he wouldn't raise his head or look up at me.

I tried to reason with him. "Honey, we love you, and we don't want you to leave us. Think how hard it'll be on Dad when he comes home tonight and you're not here." He kept looking at his shoes. "Honey, I just want you to know that if you really want to do this, any time you want to come home and play with your brothers, we'd love to have you. Besides, who's going to brush my hair? Your brothers don't know how to do that for me." "I know," he said; then, "I gotta go now." "OK," I said, and as he hugged me I told him again that I loved him. As he walked out the door with his little suitcase in his hand, he turned to look up at me and said goodbye.

"Goodbye," I replied, and slowly closed that big door behind him. He got as far as the front walk, set his case down, and sat on it. I watched him through the window as he sat there. I was getting nervous when, after about five minutes, he got up, picked up his case, came back, and rang the bell. I took my time answering. When I opened the door, he looked up at me and said, "Motho, you said I could come back and play with the boys any time I wanted?" "That's right." "OK, I want to play." He dropped his suitcase and ran to join his brothers. I kept my eyes on him the rest of the day and it appeared to me that he was fine. He completely forgot about his wanting to leave. Unbeknownst to him I unpacked his case and set it back in the closet.

When I told Jack about it that evening, he thought we should check a little further and see what made him want to leave. I felt that Patrick had put it out of his mind, and that it was best to leave well enough alone unless he tried it again. I realized that I needed to give him more attention than the other boys, so I worked at giving him special time. It's very difficult to keep everyone happy with so many boys so close in age; if one child needs more attention than the rest, he feels left out. I felt certain that such a feeling was behind this escapade, but that Patrick wasn't aware of it and he certainly wasn't alone. But he was always quick to forget, and the incident was never mentioned or repeated again.

It was then that I made plans for each boy to take me out to dinner. Jack and I discussed this at length. He felt it would be great for the boys to learn early on how to manage themselves away from home and take care of my needs while we were out at the same time. Who ever was on deck at the time of the scheduled dinner would pick the restaurant, open the car door for me, attend my chair at the restaurant, order meals for both of us, pay the check, and leave a tip, while Dad stayed home with his brothers.

It worked like a charm and the boys loved it. The personnel at the restaurants always admired the boys. I loved both the attention and care they'd give me, and the chance to talk to my son's one on one. They talked about how they felt about different things, and about what I did that met with their disapproval. They told me how I could improve my methods of training and discipline. I was able to get many good ideas from them, and often asked myself who was training whom. Amazing what a little attention can do!

During their early school years, all the childhood diseases befell the whole family at the same time. The three older boys were admitted simultaneously to Community Hospital to have their tonsils out. Thankfully, their recuperation period was very short. There was no singing then, but they kept perfectly still when I read short stories to them, and in a few days the three boys were back to normal once again.

As the five birthdays came up we loved sharing the celebrations with Dad. We always kept him informed so he'd make time for us. I'd remind him of the next birthday and tell him about our plans for the seven of us. I would inform his secretary Vera and she would take notes. When the day came, invariably Jack was working late; she would caution him that the boys and I were waiting for him and to get his carcass home. I loved how she reminded him of our needs. She not only was the greatest secretary but a great friend as well.

As Terry's fifth birthday rolled around the boys and I planned a little party for him. We decided to say nothing to him until Dad came home—hopefully, on time. As it turned out, he missed dinner and nothing had been said to our birthday boy by late evening. Just as I'd given up and was about to start the celebration, Terry took his fingers out of his mouth and sang out, "Happy birthday to me, happy birthday to me!"

And at that moment Dad finally appeared at the door. We gave Terry his presents and served ice cream with his special birthday cake. He was so happy, saying, "I thought everybody forgot me." We all chuckled, and then Terry added, "I'm sure glad you could make it after all, Dad!"

After the party Dad said, "It's late, fellows, and time to hit the sack." They protested, "Please, Dad, let us stay up a little longer!" "Remember, fellows," Dad replied, "Early to bed and early to rise, makes a man healthy, wealthy, and wise." "But Dad," said Terry, "I'm not a man yet." "Give it time, son, give it time!"

I was so dedicated to my role as a homemaker that I became a perfectionist. Regular duties never ended for me. Setting monthly schedules for the boys in order to keep them from becoming bored was a constant process. But every Sunday morning during those early years, Jack took it upon himself to get breakfast for all of us. He loved pancakes, and he'd make them very thin, the way he liked them. That was my treat from him on Sunday morning.

After breakfast we'd attend mass at Sacred Heart Catholic Church, fifteen minutes from our home. One Sunday after service we arrived home to discover that we had left Dennis behind. We were so embarrassed, but we went straight back to the church. We found Dennis, only five at the time, crying while two teenage girls held his hands. We thanked the girls and apologized to Dennis for not taking a head count before we left the church. He dried his tears as we promised we'd never allow that to happen again. "OK, thank you Mom, and you too Dad". He was such a happy camper again.

When the four boys were in school, Dennis and I spent a great deal of time together. It made no difference where we went or what we did. I kept the radio on in the car and at home, and we listened to lots of music. The song "Love and Marriage" would play many times a day, and Dennis would sing along to his heart's content bouncing back and forth with the music. Sometimes I'd sing with him. Between songs I impressed him with the idea of saying his AB'C backwards. It

wasn't long before he recited them backwards and then forwards. Z,Y
,X,W,V,U,T,S,R,Q,P,O,N,M,L,K,J,I,H,G,F,E,D,C,B,A That was quite
an accomplishment for all the boys.

Children are bound to be disappointed when there needs clash,
and at those times it was up to me to solve the problem. From
time to time, the boys would argue long and loud over whom was
wearing whose clothes. One day I couldn't stand it any longer, so
all six of us went clothes shopping at my favorite Harry Coffee's
department store. We picked items that were alike in color: shirts,
jackets, trousers, underwear, and socks. At home I immediately
laid out the new clothes in a row on the table starting with Jackie's.
I used Morse code with India ink to mark the clothes like this:

Jackie	one dot
Patrick	two dots
Terry	three dots
Michael	four dots
Dennis	one dot and a dash

The positive effect this had on the boys was tremendous. They
really loved wearing their look-alike clothes. No one dared to
wear clothes that didn't belong to him. Sorting was effortless, and
misplaced clothing was easy to find. They kept asking, "When are
we going shopping again Mom?

In our household, the importance of good manners and consideration for one another was constantly stressed. We gave each
boy a specified chore for different days of the week; not a terrible lot of work, but enough to keep them busy. I kept a chart in
the kitchen to monitor the chores. We rotated chores from month
to month, and the boys were responsible for checking off their
accomplishments. From time to time I questioned their checkmarks, but our system worked well; not only did it ensure the help
I badly needed; it also gave them pride in themselves and encouraged self-discipline. If a chore went undone, missing checkmarks
made it obvious who had forgotten what. No matter how hard they
tried, there was no escape.

This chart listed household chores, but each boy also had personal responsibilities. They had to make their own beds every
morning before breakfast, put their clean clothes in drawers and

soiled ones in the hamper, and put away their toys. Their room, and I mean room was always clean; I never had to pick up after them. At breakfast I always thanked them for this, and my simple praise went a long way.

Keeping them busy at play was equally important, and I intervened only when it got too loud or too rough. If their play seemed too exhausting, I treated them with their favorite snack—peanut butter and jelly sandwiches and milk—to smooth things down. We simply took time out, shared a treat, and talked about what we were doing and where we were going.

Michael's temper always got him into trouble when he didn't get his way. When he was upset he'd wiggle his body, breathe heavily, and make ugly noises in his throat—and the madder he'd get, the harder he'd wiggle. One Sunday afternoon when he was about six he stormed into the kitchen. I asked him what was wrong. He insisted nothing was wrong, and refused to discuss it with me. "I don't want to talk to you, Mom. You'll take the boys' side." With that he ran out of the house. I called him back, but he headed for the washroom where his father was. I grabbed Jack's belt and ran after him. When I got there Michael was wrapping his little body around Dad's legs. I let go with the belt but caught Jack, who screamed, "What are you trying to do, kill me?" I apologized as Jack picked up Michael, who was screaming, "I want to stay with you, Dad; the boys don't want to play with me!" That boy wiggled and grunted all the way back to the house.

Jack set Michael down at the kitchen table, said, "This is between you and Mother," and left us alone. I said, "You're using the wrong technique, Michael. Look at you—you're so miserable. When you get mad, the only one who's unhappy here is you. For heaven's sake, use some psychology!" "What's that?" "Agree to play, then turn the tables and inject what you want to do. You've got to be clever, and I think it'll work!" "Maybe," he said. Then Jack returned and Michael said, "How about a game of chess, Dad?" I said, "That's a great idea." Jack looked at me and said, "OK, let me wash my hands while you set up the board." I hugged Michael, told him I loved him, and asked, "Do you think you can beat Dad?" With a big smile he said, "I'm going to try."

When Michael was in Kindergarten at Chester Rowell, he like the other boys walked to and from school. One afternoon when he was on his way home a man in a black car stopped Michael. He told him that *his mother asked him to bring him home*. Michael smiled and said *"No she didn't"* and he ran home. When he arrived and explained his experience I was furious. "Where did he stop you?" "Right there on Olive." "Do you mean at Food Basket!" "Yes" I thanked him and told him he did the right thing. He said, "Yes I know." I of course reported it to the Principal at school. Most important I monitored Michael for a few days incase that man returned. Thankfully the man disappeared from our area.

Never in all those years did Jack or I ever interfere with the discipline we gave each of the boys. Going back and forth between us wasn't the answer for our sons—and they knew it. There was a time when I thought I might go crazy with all that was going on. But I persisted with my discipline and most of the time it worked. It took time but it was wear and tear on my system.

Early one morning Jack called to ask if I could help him at the office. I told Michael and Dennis to get their shoes on because Dad needed us at the office, but they were playing chess and didn't want to go. "Get your shoes on this very minute." Michael fussed all the way to the office and kept it up after we arrived. He made such a spectacle of himself I had to order him to sit in a chair until I was ready to leave. "Sit there and be quiet, or go to the car and sit. Take your choice."

Vera heard the commotion in the stockroom from her office and came out to see if she could help. As Michael continued to fuss, wiggling in his seat, Vera tried to console him. "Michael, your mother doesn't mean to be harsh with you; she just wants to help your father. I'll tell you what: If you want to, you can come home with me and be my little boy for a while. Would you like that?"

Michael looked up and said harshly, "What's the matter with you, Vera, aren't you ever going to get married and have children of your own?" Vera bowed her head and walked back to her office. I was working in the stock room and heard Michael. I was stunned, and embarrassed. Before we left the office I apologized for my son's behavior. Vera said it was Ok, she understood. But I didn't.

When we arrived home I ordered him to his room to think about what he'd said to Vera. "The way you talked to her was unforgivable. You embarrassed me. You're not allowed to leave your room until you can apologize to me for your actions. And the next time we go to Dad's office I want you to apologize to Vera for being so rude to her! Is that understood? I'm so ashamed of you."

Just so Michael wouldn't forget we appeared at the office in a couple of days. My son flooded Vera with compliments before he offered his apology. In his own little way he was so polished. He knew how to turn the tables making him look good before offering any apology. She was extremely gracious as she accepted with a grin. "Thank you, Mike, I understand."

It wasn't every night that the boys were lucky enough to have their father tuck them into bed, so when he wasn't home I made it a habit to talk about the next day's activities. They'd let their hair down and relate their plans to see what I thought. Where they got all their ideas was a mystery to me. As it turned out, before they fell asleep they were looking forward to the next day.

Many times in the evening and after much conversation to get the boys relaxed, Dad and I would sing one of their favorite songs before they closed their eyes. One of Dad's favorites, and he had many, was "I'll Get By." He'd hold my hand and really ham it up, and sometimes I'd sing good behavior. A goodnight kiss made them happy, and all was quiet on the home front again. Amen!

Chapter 12

In the Good Old Summertime

*L*ife took on a different quality in the summer. For many years we had a little swimming pool. When the heat was unbearable, I'd fill it with water and the boys would jump in to keep cool. One day, before Dennis was born, I took a priceless picture of the four boys playing in the pool. When the film had been developed, Kodak Company chose it as the picture of the month. It was enlarged to an eight-by-ten print, framed, and posted at the camera store for everyone to see. At the end of the month it was given to us as a keepsake. I had it specially framed and I still treasure it.

In those days everything seemed so expensive, and those boys ate everything in sight. To save money, one summer Mrs. Syvertsen taught me how to can fresh fruit. During canning season the boys were allowed in the house only to use the bathroom or to take something from their room that they needed outside. We'd eat our lunch out on the patio; it was different, and fun to do.

Our apricot tree always produced fruit in abundance, and I wasted not one apricot. The boy's loved pure apricot preserves, so I prepared jars for family use plus a special pint jar for each boy with his name on it. We feasted on apricot jam that year, and when the family jars were empty we all hoped to be invited to share in the personal jars. They didn't have to share if they didn't want to, and how they would tease each of us before they would pass their own jar around!

When I wasn't canning, I had to devise activities for the boys. Their chores weren't enough to keep them busy; they'd get bored and cause distractions and arguments. One year I called a special conference at the beginning of summer. I told the boys we needed to put our heads together about what we were going to do that summer. Everybody had to agree, and if we couldn't make a decision, we'd stay home and work. There was much discussion, and it was a treat to hear the ideas these boys came up with.

We finally decided that they would take turns deciding what to do. Jackie went first, choosing what we'd all do for the day; then the next day Patrick would get to choose, and so on. Each agreed to do what the others wanted on their days, knowing that soon each of them would choose their activity. Happily, there was never an argument; it turned out to be a great plan that worked every time. With five boys making choices, we did so many interesting things.

We went to the movies, swimming, shopping, and to the park with special lunches for birthday celebrations. They conjured up so many ideas and I loved it. Jackie noted that someday he, too, would be able to drive us around. I'm not sure how we managed without Dad sometimes. He never argued about the cost, but we always tried to be conservative.

Jack's passion was golf and he joined a special club for us. The Fort Washington Golf Club, in the remote town of Pinedale, California that included a beautiful restaurant and two swimming pools—a small pool for little tykes like Dennis and a big one for adults and experienced swimmers. Since Jackie, Pat, and Terry had taken swimming lessons, they felt they could handle the big pool with no problem. They all loved the water, and were all fair swimmers—except Patrick, who swam like a fish—and that was good enough for me. Michael and Dennis had to wear life jackets, and I'd take them into the shallow pool and teach them how to kick, float, dog paddle, and hold their breath underwater. Michael loved the big pool so much; it was all I could do to keep track of him. He had his life jacket on, and as he became a little more experienced I didn't worry.

We'd enjoy the pool during the day; while we waited for the evening when we could all have dinner with their father. Many times Jack met us at the Fort after a round of golf. Patrick would stand on the edge of the course wishing he could play, too. When I told Jack about this, he informed Patrick that he had to be seven years old before he could even walk the course. It seemed unfair to him, but those were the rules. Pat accepted this with a smile, but bowed his head in disappointment. He had the same passion as his father, but I told him the time would fly fast, Dad would soon teach him how to putt, but in the meantime we would have fun at Fort Washington.

Two months before the end of one summer, the four older boys were having a great time on the diving board. Dennis was so envious that, without my noticing it, he ventured down to the deep end of the pool without his life jacket on. Patrick and Dennis looked so much alike in those days that, when I looked over at the diving board, I thought I was watching Patrick. As he ran to the end of the diving board I realized my mistake, and screamed "Dennis!" when he leaped into the air. Fortunately, Terry and Jackie saw Dennis hit the water and watched for him to surface. They flanked Dennis and pushed him as he dog-paddled to the ladder where Pat and Michael helped him out of the pool. By that time I was there with a towel.

As I dried him off I asked why he would try such a trick. "All the boys were having so much fun and I wanted to have fun, too," was his response. "When you hit the water and went under, what were you thinking?" I demanded. I was still shaken. Serenely Dennis told me, "Remember when you told me to hold my breath if I ever fell in deep water, because the water would bring me to the surface? Well, I wanted to see if it was really true." Thank God for small favors. I then made Dennis promise me he would never do that until he was an experienced swimmer.

Our family gatherings were few and far between. Grandpa Nutter and Emma (Jack's father and his second wife) would come to visit us in the late summer from Concordia, Kansas. They'd spend at least two weeks with us and Grandpa would go to work with Jack every day. My friend Margie Rodgers and her husband, Ed, would come over in the evening and the men would play pitch (a Kansas card game) and drink red wine. Margie, Emma and I would go to the movies, leaving the men to baby sit. Arriving home after the movies the boys were laughing so hard about their game and we roared at their red teeth and purple lips. How they loved the wine.

Each one of the boys had a chance to visit Grandpa and Emma on the farm in Kansas during early summer vacation. They loved the importance it gave them as they boarded United Airlines heading for the wild blue yonder and for their grandfather's farm. Our sentimental goodbyes were never easy.

Early in Jackie's life he asked if he and his brothers could go to a summer camp for Catholic boys in Watsonville, California. Jack and I decided it would be a good experience for the four older boys. We cautioned them about the different personalities they'd confront, and how they could deal with them. The boys were intrigued and eager to go. Their experiences were so positive that summer camp became part of our annual schedule.

One year Jack asked if there was a chance that Dennis could go, too. He was not quite eight, too young for camp, but we figured that since his four brothers were going, we just might get the administrator's approval. Jack was feeling neglected; he wanted us to have time alone together, and I too felt that was a good idea. I loved spending time alone with my husband. I was able to get the administrators approval, so that summer I bought new jeans, shirts, and white tennis shoes for five boys instead of just four.

As we headed for Watsonville that year, I casually explained to Dennis in the car that he needn't discuss his age with anyone. When we arrived, Jack and I dropped each of the older boys at their respective bungalows and said our goodbyes. Dennis was last, and since this was his first time at camp, we went with him into his bungalow. We spotted Father Steve, the administrator, talking to some boys. Jack introduced Dennis and I to Father, who took one look at Dennis, put his big hand on our son's head, and said, "Tell me, young man, how old are you really?" My mouth flew open with shock! Dennis looked up at Father, stuck his right foot forward on the floor as he twisted it a little, and said, "I'm not sure, Father; I'm just as confused about my age as my parents are."

The three of us chuckled but said our goodbyes quickly; Jack ushered me out saying, "Honey, would you please look up his birth certificate and get his birthday straight!" When we were safely in the car I told my husband, "Dennis is two years younger than Michael—and you know very well why he's here so early!" We drove home laughing about Father's remark and feeling that Dennis had handled himself very well.

After having had hardwood floors for years, Jack and I decided to have wall-to-wall carpeting installed throughout the house.

While the boys were gone we relished the idea of just sitting on the new carpeting or lying down with a pillow watching television or reading. A luxury we were unable to afford in the beginning stages. It was heaven and Jack was ever so happy with just the two of us.

San Joaquin High School had an Olympic-size swimming pool, and from time to time I'd treat the boys to a swim while I watched. One day Patrick made a swan dive from the high board. I thrilled as he flew into the air and hit the water like a knife. It was perfect; not one little splash. When he surfaced, everyone around the pool cheered and applauded. Nothing could have pleased him more and he bowed as he said, "Thank You!"

Going to the movies was my favorite pastime and it was music to my ears when my boys wanted to go. I'd often forget where I'd parked the car, but Patrick had such a good sense of direction that he'd always steer us exactly where the car was parked. We'd then head for our favorite restaurant for dinner. Jackie would open the car door for me; Patrick would open the restaurant door; Terry would help me with my chair in the restaurant; and Michael would take my napkin, snap it open, and place it on my lap with a flourish. He was such a ham.

For one of our excursions we set our sights on the Ambassador Hotel on Wilshire Boulevard in Los Angeles for lunch. As Patrick walked ahead to open the big beautiful door, it swung open automatically just as he hit the electronic beam. He stood there for a moment, then turned to us and said, "Now that's what I call service!" He watched delightedly as the door closed behind us. "I love this!" he said. He was seven at the time.

The boys chose one of several restaurants, and we took our place in line. The hostess escorted us to very nice table with a view. She gave us our menus and spoke briefly to each boy. The first thing that caught the boys' eyes on that menu was the cost of the entrees. Jackie looked at me and said, "Mom, can we afford this? We don't mind leaving if you don't have enough cash." Each boy agreed. I responded confidently, "It's OK; surely I have enough to see us through. We just won't be able to do this very often." I felt this was a healthy way to communicate with my boys, and to strengthen our family bond. It's great to do something a little expensive once in a while.

No matter where we dined, the boys never forgot to express themselves politely with "Thank you," "Excuse me," "I'm sorry," and most of all "Please." These words were instilled in them from the day they first started to talk. I'd often tell my sons how much I appreciated their behavior away from home, especially when friends call to ask me what I'd done to create such well-mannered boys. Each of them made their father and me proud as the years rolled by.

Very often I was told that I was lucky to have such well-mannered sons. Lucky no, I simply made my luck. It was a constant course of action. Dad and I set the example we wanted the boys to follow and that was easy and natural for them. In essence to mold those little bodies from their beginning was the greatest of all ventures for both Dad and I. Never a day would go by but what I wasn't proud of their actions. There were times when I knew that these boys were even proud of go by, themselves.

An 8x10 "Picture of the Month" voted by Kodak and posted on the wall above the Drug store counter in 1954

Easter Sunday at Rodeing Park Patrick's back, Terry, Jackie and Michael kneeling 1953

Our back yard as we were ready to Leave for the "Fresno Fair." Jackie Patrick, Terry and Michael.

Chapter 13

The Silent Treatment

I have never been one to complain of a little pain here or there; what ever it is, it'll go away. But late 1954 I came to realize something was wrong. It became difficult to swallow my own saliva, and food seemed to stick in my throat. Eventually it would go down, but eating was so painful that I avoided food as much as I could. If I talked too much, my throat would hurt immensely. These symptoms got progressively worse, but as usual I simply waited for them to go away. Then one morning I found that my clothes were falling off my hips, so I weighed myself. For years I'd tipped the scales between 105 and 108, but this time I weighed in at 89 pounds. I was losing too much too fast, and the pain in my throat was almost too much to bear. I had to do something.

I needed to consult a doctor, but had no idea whom to see. I didn't want to burden our friends with worry if there was anything drastically wrong, so Marvin (our Ears Nose & Throat doctor friend) wasn't an option. My pride really got the best of me, but I decided to deal with telling Jack and the boys when I knew what was wrong. I chose a nearby physician out of the telephone directory Dr. Davis.

My appointment was on a Friday. My interview went well, but the exam didn't. The doctor did little to put me at ease, and failed several times to insert an instrument deep in my throat because I gagged uncontrollably. I was frustrated and felt he should do better, but I said nothing. He apologized and prescribed medication to be taken twice a day that would relax my throat. I was rescheduled for the following Monday afternoon to try again. Still I decided to say nothing to dad.

I started the medication that evening. It did nothing for the pain; and worse, within 24 hours it threw me into a terrible state of depression. It was so intense that I wanted to kill myself. I knew immediately it had to be the prescribed drug that was causing the problem. I stopped the medication intending to notify the doctor early Monday morning. This was not working for me. There had to be a better way.

Very early Monday morning Dr. Davis's nurse called me to make an appointment with a different doctor. It was too much for me; hysteria crept in and I went wild on the phone, certain that the end was near. The nurse finally managed to calm me down and explained that my doctor had died of a heart attack over the weekend. Stunned, I apologized for my behavior and expressed my deepest sympathy.

The appointment with my new physician Dr. Bacon was a much better experience. He was such an endearing man, kind and very gentle in his voice, manner, and touch. I was so relaxed and calm during our interview, after which he explained briefly what he needed to do. He put a piece of gauze on my tongue pulled down, and before I had time to think, the instrument was deep in my throat. I was so impressed; I could barely feel the instrument but best of all no gagging. As he examined my throat, he murmured, "For Heaven's sake," and then, "This is very interesting." When the tool ascended and he released my tongue, I was so relaxed and feeling so proud of myself. I wanted to stand up and cheer.

"I can see that this has been a real problem for you," he said. I nodded, and he asked permission to take another look. Again I nodded. When he finished he set his instrument down. I anxiously asked what he'd found, and he replied, "My dear, you have what we commonly call *Ulcers of the Vocal Cords*. There's a medical term for it, but in essence, this is what you have."

As simply as he could, he explained that I had blisters at the end of my vocal cords, a very painful and quite common condition for which there is only one cure. Nervously, I asked if he meant an operation, and was both relieved and confused when his answer was NO! He then told me I needed complete rest—no speaking, no housework, no stress—and recommended that I go away by myself for six months. I couldn't believe he was serious!

"You don't understand, Doctor. I have five sons who need me, and only two of them are in school. My husband has to work, and I simply can't go off alone. Aside from that, we can't afford such an expense. There has to be another way!"

Gently he replied, "Please go home; talk to your husband and your children. If you don't accept this cure you will, in all probability, get worse, and somewhere down the road this could develop into something more serious. I want to see you six months from today." He saw the pain in my face, the tears in my eyes and immediately added, "There's no other way. I can, however, promise you an almost complete recovery if you decide to work this out."

I thanked him as the nurse made my appointment for six months. As I left the office in a mild state of shock, I kept asking myself, "How, dear God, how?" I don't remember driving home; all I remember is that I needed to do something. I called Jack's office; when Vera answered she asked how I was feeling, I fibbed and said fine. Jack was out and I told her he needn't return my call, but it was vitally important that he be home for dinner at six o'clock.

I then summoned the little boys from their play. I told them they needed to be washed and ready for dinner at six. When the two older boys came home from school I told them we'd all have dinner tonight in the dining room. "Must be something important," Jackie said. As casually as I could, I said, "Yes, it's very important honey, so please be ready on time." They all agreed.

Jack arrived at six o'clock, and the boys managed to be ready without any fuss. I could sense them all watching me curiously, but nevertheless we ate by candlelight and in complete silence. They kept looking up from time to time, but no one said a word. Dad's curiosity got the best of him toward the end of dinner. "OK, Mom, what's this all about?"

I fought back the tears with all my might. It was so difficult to even talk. I began by telling dad and the boys that I had gone to see an ENT (Ear and Nose & Throat) doctor that day. Yes, dad said with a questionable tone in his voice. When I was able to explain my dilemma and recount what the doctor's impossible cure was, a complete silence hovered over the table. Dad got up from his chair, walked over and kneeled beside me, and said, "Honey, I've known for quite some time that you haven't been feeling too good, but I thought it was because the boys have been too much for you. I was thinking seriously of getting some daily help for you."

"Please honey, that's not it," I said. He held me in his arms as I proceeded to dry my tears. He was at a loss for words. He hung his head as if he were to blame for my illness. I put my arms around him and told him not to feel bad; it is not his fault. It's only me!

"Well, fellows," he said as he stood beside me, "What do we do? Mom really needs help. Can anyone offer a solution? How can we possibly let her leave us for any length of time?"

The tears were flowing down my cheeks when Dennis, just a baby then, came over and hugged me and told me how much he loved me. When he said, "Don't cry, Mommy," my heart very nearly broke. Jackie piped up, "I have the answer for you, Mom," and Patrick said, "Please don't cry, Mom. We're here for you. Let's see what Jack has to say."

Our number-one son had plenty to say. "You don't have to go anywhere. We're not going to let you talk. We boys are going to take care of you. We can do it," as his brothers, chorused their approval.

"How?" I asked miserably. "Dad has to work, and you and Patrick have school every day. The rest of you boys are babies. Besides, there's so much work involved here at the house."

"School will be out in a month, Mom. Whenever you need us to do something, just write us a note. No talking, just rest. Remember, Mom, we already have our chores to do, and we will do them. You don't have to worry. If the doctor wants you to rest, then rest is what you'll get."

Everybody agreed it was a great idea. Then Dad spoke up. "Do you boys really think you can work this out? I'll help with breakfast and get you boys off to school in the morning. I'll call Mrs. Syvertsen to come over in the afternoon to look after things and get lunch for the little guys, and she can get dinner started for us. She's a great cook and I know she'd love to help. What do you think?"

"Look fellows," I interrupted, "I want all of you to listen to me. This treatment, according to the doctor, will take at least six months. Do you understand how long and how slow six months can be? Besides that, I'm not too sure that I can keep my mouth shut that long." It will be difficult for all of us and especially for you honey.

Dad said firmly, "Now you listen to me, Mom. I really think we need to give this a try. We're not going to let you down and we certainly aren't going to let you talk. For you to be away from us for that long would only worry us. This is a simple answer, and an unusual answer, so how about it? You're the boss. Will you cooperate with us?"

All the boys chimed in. "We can do it, Mom. Please, let us prove it to you. We've always needed you and you were there; now you need us, and here we are. Anyway, you can't go any place without us, you know that."

That did it; I thought for a second, smiled, and said, "I'll give it a try." The outpouring of love and affection was so endearing, how could I not make the effort? The thought of not having to leave them was my greatest relief.

Every commitment I had outside of our home, from socializing with friends to participating in church activities, came to a standstill while I concentrated on getting better. Just keeping calm and resting was very hard for me. Mrs. Syvertsen was so great about making special foods. I could drink only with a spoon, and she made sure a glass of fresh cold water was constantly at my side. My throat would get very dry and the water helped a lot. All I could think was six months; I've got to do it.

At times when I tried to do something, the little boys would grab my hand, look up at me, and usher me back to the couch. They designed special paper notes for me to write on, and a pencil never left my side. Terry would look up at me, shake his finger with one hand, and suck two fingers on the other hand if I tried to do anything. It wasn't that I wanted to do anything; it simply was very hard on me to just sit around.

Patrick would get home from school before Jackie and ask me how I was feeling, then immediately put his hand over my mouth and hand me a pencil and tablet. My hair was very long then and he loved to brush it. He'd brush very slowly so as not to pull, and when he was through he'd bend down, kiss my cheek and ask, "You feel better now?" I'd nod and he'd smile. I loved watching him check on the little boys; it made him feel so important. He'd make tea for me before Dad came home and he did it with a smile, making sure it was cool before it touched my lips. Mrs. Syvertsen always had hot water ready for him; she knew how he loved to bring it to me. He wanted to do his part. It was such a great feeling knowing how much he and the boys cared.

When Jackie would come home he'd check on everybody, making sure everything was running smoothly. He'd sit in front of me and tell me about things at school. His performance at school was such that I got only good reports about him. I was so proud of his thoughtfulness and his eagerness to excel. I never had to tell him to study. He loved school and always got along with his classmates.

Dad was home early most of the time so that he could finalize dinner for the boys. He called Mrs. Syvertsen every day to check on me, and to say he was *thinking of me and that loved me.* Mrs. S. always delighted in giving me this message.

The time came when I felt sorry for myself. How could I have allowed this to happen? Where did I go wrong? What could I have done to prevent this? It was a very difficult time, but I never let my feelings of depression reach the boys' eyes or ears. That would be letting them down and would make them feel bad, so I was very cautious.

After Jack had the boys ready for bed they'd all come to kiss me goodnight and tell me how much they loved me. Their love really made my day. When our sons were asleep, I'd shower and go to bed, where Dad would hold me in his arms for the longest time. He'd ask questions I could answer with a nod or a shake, and tell me how the boys prayed for me every night. The day I started my cure he had begun marking the calendar with a big X on each day of my silent therapy. Every night he'd say so many days down and so many to go, and ask if I believed I was making progress. I'd nod and he'd squeeze me tight, and he would tell me *he loved me, and then he would say, "I know you love me, too honey."* Those were trying times for him, but he was such a comfort and how I loved him in return.

When Dad had to go away for a couple of days, he'd call to check up on the little guys, and he and the boys would confer about my progress. There was never a problem with them. They would play chess or checkers to their hearts' content, and that kept them very busy and very quiet. Dad had started all the boys on chess from the age of three. He also told them that he would teach them, but he would not let them casually win. They had to do that on their own. It amazed me how quickly they caught on.

I don't believe I could have had any better care with anyone else. Being close to my family was healing enough for me. Their thoughtfulness, consideration, and love pulled me through. The little boys each had something special to do for me during the day while the older boys were in school.

Michael took over the responsibilities of his younger brothers. Now he was king of the household. When he thought I was napping, he'd come over, check me out, and motion for everyone to be quiet, whispering that I was asleep. How thoughtful! He was only 4.

In the afternoon Terry and Michael constantly played chess. They loved the game and each one tried to out due the other. I was ever so glad the boys enjoyed such a quiet game! Dennis would sit quietly with me on the couch, holding my hand and watching his brothers. Those were peaceful and tender times. How could I not get well?

After about four months I started to feel much better. I had hardly any pain in my throat; I could drink without a straw or spoon, and enjoy soft foods again. I was so excited that I really wanted to talk, but I didn't. A couple more weeks went by and I continually felt better. When Mrs. Syvertsen came one morning I motioned to her that I wanted to talk. She immediately checked the calendar, reported that it had only been four months and so many days, and reminded me what the doctor said. I knew she was right. Two weeks later I was up to 99 pounds and feeling great, so Mrs. S. made an appointment for me. It gave me renewed hope. I showered and for the first time in all those months (which seemed like an eternity) I had enough energy to apply make-up.

The doctor was his usual charming self. He said I looked great and looked rested and asked only yes-or-no questions. As he prepared to descend down my throat, I prayed fervently. He checked me out thoroughly and then said, "I really want you to give it another three weeks at least. Looks great so far, but more rest is of the essence. Let's not rush this!" I was disappointed, but obedient; I had come too far to hinder my health now. What was another three weeks? Yes I can do it.

When I got home the little boys ushered me to the couch. Mrs. S. had lunch for me and asked no questions. She knew by the look on my face what the doctor said.

At the end of those three weeks the doctor re-evaluated my condition. I kept my eyes on his face as he probed my throat. I could see he was pleased and I was thrilled, especially since I was feeling so good. His next words nearly made me giddy: "Your throat looks almost perfect. You're free to talk."

"It's important for you to realize," he continued, "that when this type of blister heals it causes scarring. You have scars at the end of your vocal cords, and more than likely, they will never go away. The blisters can reappear, depending on how much you speak and the tone of your voice. You'll tire easily. Talking on the phone as you're lying down creates pressure on your vocal cords, and it'll be uncomfortable for you. Singing high notes will be difficult, and singing for long periods of time will tire you immensely and be painful. That's the penalty for this type of illness."

I was so happy to have my life back again with such few restrictions! I knew I could take it. I said, "I feel so good right now, and I plan to keep it that way." The sound of my voice was no different than before. I told the doctor about Jack and our boys and all they did for me. He congratulated me on my accomplishment and marveled over my sons. I told him they were my saviors and that my husband had been ever so patient with me, expecting nothing but patience in return. I talked about Jack's wise assessment of my condition and the loving way he encouraged me every day, and the doctor said that he, too, needed to be congratulated. We said our goodbyes and I never had to appear in his office again. The cure took just over five and a half months—a blessing from God and the patience of my family.

That evening Mrs. Syvertsen assisted me with a special dinner for the family. It was hard to believe how tired I got just sitting around. Jack knew I'd seen the doctor that day and came home early. The boys were washed and seated at the table, anxious for good news. All eyes were upon me, and it was Dad who couldn't wait any longer and asked, "Do you have some good news for us, Mom?" Very clearly, in my own voice, I said to them, "The doctor tested me today and gave me a clean bill of health and a full pardon!"

The smiles on every face were a sight to behold. Mrs. Syvertsen beamed as she served my equally radiant family. I said I'd been giving a great deal of thought to our future, and that our rules were changing. "I bought a whistle today before coming home," I said, and showed them it was hanging around my neck. "From now on, the minute this whistle sounds out, all of you boys are to make your appearance on the back patio immediately. The whistle will become my voice when I need you." The boys were so happy to hear me they would've agreed to anything. And Dad, so proud of my improvement, agreed to help me to enforce the new rule. I was so proud of myself I wanted to stand up and cheer.

With my next breath I said my recovery was due to their patience, and I wanted them to know how much I appreciated their support and I loved each one of them for this. They'd all made sacrifices, but I would make it up to them in the months to come. Emotions were high on all sides, and then Dad said, "OK, guys, let's do our thing." He motioned to Dennis to come forward. As he did Jackie handed him a package under the table. Dennis presented me with a gift of a beautiful white embroidered blouse, saying, "This comes from all of us, Mom." Dad came over and knelt beside me and said, with a big hug and a kiss, "All of us; we love you so much and we want you to stay well and happy." I said, "Thank you honey and I love you too." Looking around to the boys, I said, and I love each and every one of you too.

Evening prayers were very special that night. The boys couldn't thank God enough for all his help in renewing my health, and I thanked him for giving me such great sons as I hugged and kissed each one good night.

Thankfully, it was time to move on. I don't suppose I could ever measure how hard this really was on my family. Especially on Jack, because I know he worried about me. Not one of the boys ever complained about the confinement. Certainly there was no vacation time, and by the time I was on the move again, school had started and Terry entered kindergarten.

Dad's love and endearing ways made me comfortable and happy to be alive. I was proud of his encouragement and the support he gave me as I started to feel better. We were a happy family and it was up to me to keep that way.

Chapter 14

Not the Same Old Song and Dance

*O*nce my cure was complete, I threw myself into my life with zest and enthusiasm. I felt good and my spirits were very high. It was the fall of 1954 and the boys were back in school again. It felt like a fresh new start.

Prior to my becoming ill I had inquired about enrolling Jackie in tap-dancing classes. Now I felt the need to make up for lost time. He took a class once a week without fail. He seemed content with this, and it turned out he really knew how to click those taps. I never had to ask him to practice and he was always ready to go to class without my reminding him. The time came when I asked him if he'd like to teach me a step or two. "Sure, Mom, if you want to learn, I can teach you." He demonstrated steps that were easy enough and he was an excellent teacher.

He was impressed with what he taught me, and he told me so. I would take a short bow in thanks. Some time later we competed with each other and had fun doing it. His dance lessons lasted for almost seven years, with recitals at the end of each year. He performed with his class and he performed solos on stage, often wearing costumes I'd made for him.

Jackie and Patrick were both Cub Scouts, and Dad was their troop's Cub Master. Jackie was asked to perform at a Scout meeting, and planned a dance to "That Old Black Magic." He knew the routine well, but that night for some reason he got cold feet. As I was preparing to play his music, he called me over and told me he was scared. I told him I was, too. That surprised him, and seemed to comfort him as well, because he said, "Don't worry, Mom, I'll be OK." As he danced he watched me out of the corner of his eye with a grin on his face, and I smiled back approvingly. From that time on it never bothered him to perform.

Dad and I found an old upright piano in excellent condition and had it delivered to the house. When the older boys came home from school they stared at it without a word. At dinner that night I announced that whoever was interested in learning how to play that piano all they had to do was to speak up, or forever hold their peace. Michael and Terry showed definite interest and I promptly enrolled them in regular lessons. Both boys loved the piano and spent many hours pounding away at the keyboard. Terry couldn't pass it without pausing, looking, and then his finger would hit the ole eighty-eight and he'd play to his heart's content. But it was only a passing fancy for him; his real interest was *WRITING*.

Patrick took voice lessons for a while; it was natural for him but not a challenge. In his opinion anybody could sing, and he soon lost interest. He then decided that he wanted to play drums, and Dad and I bought a beautiful set of white chrome drums. He worked on them for a while, but it wasn't long before he lost interest there as well. Pat found his calling in golf. At first I didn't take it very serious, but it turned out that he'd do anything that would place him on the golf course. I delighted in watching him hit a ball exactly where he'd told me to look. He had such control with the clubs—and he was only twelve at the time.

Then there was Dennis. He also took piano although he didn't stay with it either. His forte was the trumpet. I found him a Constellation Trumpet, reputed to be a superior instrument, and he was impressed with it. After the noise wasn't noise any more, I really liked the sounds that came out of that horn.

A few years later, after we'd left Fresno, Dennis and some of his friends put a band together. They named themselves the "Crimson Tide" and would practice regularly. Jackie's friend Danny played the drums in his own band, but he'd come over and join the boys' practice often. It was good clean fun—but it sure was loud!

Over a period of time, I realized that for me to have any kind of influence over the boys, I would need to be very patient with them. If Jack didn't mind the cost of all these experiments, far be it from me to discourage anything that our sons aspired to do. As long as they did it within reason I could see nothing wrong. I knew the day would come soon enough when they would realize their true calling.

While we're on the subject of Jack, I must tell you about an incident that really took the wind out of my sails. This was one of those days that were absolutely horrendous. All day long there was something going on with the boys, and none of it was good. There was constant discipline for one or the other, and by the time dinner came around I was completely exhausted. The boys washed and sat very quietly at the dinner table. Seeing their shining, innocent-looking faces, one would hardly believe what a difficult day we'd just been through. I found myself telling them if tomorrow was like today, they'd all be kneeling in corners. I was so upset that my words were very strong. I found no humor in anything that day and they knew it. During my tongue-lashing Dad walked in. I cut my words short when he tapped me on the shoulder and motioned me to follow him. I told the boys not to move, I'll be right back.

Jack ushered me back to the bedroom, shut the door behind me and he said in a very simply soft tone, "I don't know the reason for your harsh words as the boys were looking up at you, but I just want to tell you that right now, *you're looking down on them*, but the day will come when *they will be looking down on you*. Just keep that in mind for future days like this."

"Oh, that's great honey," I said. "You come home after work, not knowing what's gone on all day with these young sons of yours, and you proceed to call me on the carpet. In plain words, Mr. Nutter, I have had a day to end all days. These young men of ours keep trying my patience. When I say no they do their level best to get me to say yes. They wear me out. It's fight, fight, fight. "Tell me, what should I do?" When the day comes that I give in every time they want their way, what do you suppose will happen eventually? I'm not so sure that my judgment is right any more. I'm really getting tired of preaching. When these boys grow up they're going to hate me."

Jack said, "No, they'll never hate you, as long as you're fair with them." "Great," I shot back. "That's easy for you to say." We both gave a sigh of relief and returned to the kitchen. As we did ten little eyes were upon me. I could sense their anxiety. Dinner prayer was short and sweet. The boys were very polite, saying thank you, please, or you're welcome. Not another word was spoken at the table, and afterwards only "Thanks, Mom." What a switch! I did nothing the rest of the evening; Dad and the boys did the chores. Evening prayer was so special. Hugs and kisses prevailed with their apologies for the difficult day. Jackie said, "Tomorrow will be your day mom, right guys. You just tell us what you want us to do. OK Mom." With a smile I kissed each one and said, "Thanks guys. They always knew how to get to me!

Five Nutter Boys displaying their Fireman Hats. They are positioned As though they were watering down a fire.
Jackie 12, Patrick 11, Terry 10, Michael 9, Dennis 7 years.

1957

Jackie Wilcox Nutter Jr.
Ten Years Old

Patrick James Nutter
Nine Years Old

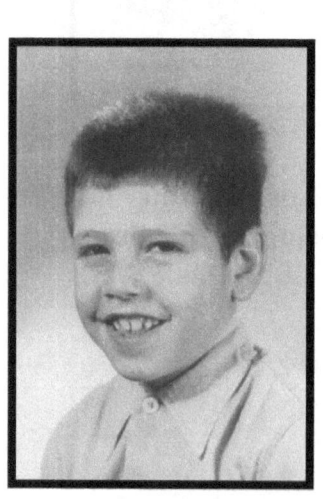

Terrill Mark Nutter
Eight Years Old

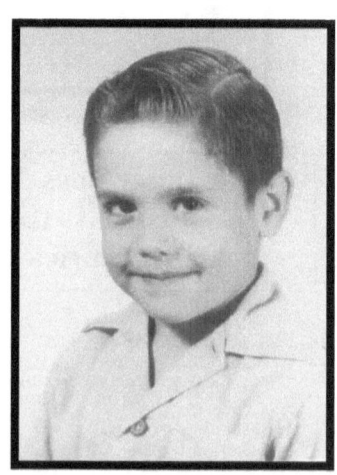

Michael Gregory Nutter
Seven Years Old

Single School Pictures above taken at Sacred Heart School

Chapter 15

Future Aspirations and Family Friends

*J*ack was a chain smoker. He always seemed to have a cigarette in his hand or hanging out of his mouth. He'd puff harder and stronger when he was angry or upset. One morning I noticed the walls were turning gray. Upon close inspection I realized both they and the curtains were stained with nicotine, and I knew I'd have to wash the walls and more than likely paint them, too.

Once in a while Dad would like to come home for lunch and this was one of those days. I told him that I wanted to show him my discovery. I demonstrated by wiping the wall with a wet towel. He couldn't believe how dirty the walls were. He had a cigarette in his hand, and he took a long drag, walked out to the backyard next to the huge tree, took another two puffs, threw the cigarette on the ground, and crushed it out with his shoe. He walked back to the house where I was watching him, and said, "You'll never have to worry about my smoking again."

I didn't believe him, but as it turned out he never touched another cigarette. A few months later, I realized that he really had stopped smoking and I asked him if he missed his cigarettes. He replied, "Yes, very much, but if I ever take another cigarette, I'd never stop again. I'm through with smoking." The lack of smoke in the house was such a blessing. I dearly respected and loved him for making that sacrifice. It took me two weeks to get our walls and curtains back to normal.

A friend of ours bought Jackie a model airplane kit for his eighth birthday. Jackie put the model together by sheer logic. He became so fascinated with building models that I bought him not only model planes but boats as well. He took good care of them for the longest time; for all I know he still has one or two.

During that time I began asking him what he thought he might want to do when he grew up. He proudly announced that he wanted to learn how to fly a plane. I told him that it would take a lot of study before he could accomplish that, possibly even years. "No matter, I have plenty of time and I can wait," was his reply.

That was when I decided to start keeping records for the boys. In October 1955 I wrote their names in a small binder. At our next conference I told them my idea of recording each of their future ambitions and aspirations. The older boys thought it was an excellent idea and they put on their thinking caps when I asked what they thought they'd like to do when they grew up. (Dennis was only three at the time, but he sat in on the meetings and listened to every word.) As each boy enthusiastically told me what he wanted to do, I recorded my first journal entrée:

Jackie	Pilot
Patrick	Catholic Priest
Terry	Pianist
Michael	Garbage Collector

At Michael's age, his choice seemed the ideal profession. Once a week, he'd sit on the back fence and visit with the garbage collector, talking about various things and asking questions. Michael was so impressed with this man that he'd watch for him down the alley on collection day. If Michael forgot, the man would call out a big "Hi, Mike!" and our son would run to visit with him. Mike announced that he had four other brothers, and all of them had daily chores except the baby. "That's great Mike." "Yes Dad says we have to help our Mom."

When Michael announced what he wanted to do, the other boys laughed. "That's OK," I said, believing he'd change his mind before long. Michael liked to get all dressed up in a suit, a Stetson hat, and polished shoes at a very young age. On some of our special outings he really looked sharp, and I admired his pride in his appearance. He had a young slim figure short in stature, but mighty in his mind.

Each year I'd bring out the journal, meet with the boys in the study, and ask the same question: "Have you given any more thought as to what you want to do when you get older?" The second year everybody's thoughts were the same except Terry's. He'd decided he wanted to be a journalist, so I changed "pianist" to "writer" and dated the change.

At our third meeting, when Dennis was five, I asked him the big question, and he replied, "Gosh, Mom, I didn't think you'd ever ask!" "Ok fellows lets listen to Dennis." As I wrote the date in the binder, Dennis said, "I ____I'm going to be a husband."

The roar of his brothers' laughter really disappointed him. "Dennis, anybody can be a husband," Michael said loudly, and everyone agreed. "Just a minute," I said. "Yes, you're right, anybody can be a husband, but not everybody can be a *good* husband." Dennis smiled and thanked me, looked around at his brothers, and said, "And don't forget that, you guys!" I recorded Dennis' choice, hugged him, and ended the meeting.

During my years of attending Mothers' Club activities at school for the boys, Jack and I got to know the different club members and as a result we developed a group of close, well-loved friends. Among them were Dr. Marvin Simmons and his wife, Gwen, who did a great deal of traveling all over the world; Willard and Isabelle Ayers, who were in the furniture business and owned one cabin in Yosemite National Park and one at Bass Lake, California; then there was Lee Silton and her husband, Joe, who worked for a company that marketed beef jerky. The eight of us was always on the receiving end of his samples.

At the end of every month, we would get together for dinner in one of our homes. After dinner we women would work on our projects from school while the men played poker, and then we would serve dessert at around midnight—the bewitching hour. The men "donated" their poker winnings to a specially decorated jar, which was transferred from one home to the next. Every September was "birthday month" and four of us had birthdays in September or October. Once a year, usually in October, the jar would "treat" all eight of us to dinner at our favorite restaurant— usually the Desert Inn Restaurant and there was always money left over for the following year. Our doctor friend, Marvin, playfully maintained that he paid for everyone's dinner each year, because he was the one who constantly lost money every time they played. He simply could not keep tract of the cards, and always made the wrong choice.

We all looked forward to these dinners, which went on for many years. Our families spent holidays together, and our celebrations were always lively and exciting—between the four couples we sprouted fifteen children in eight years. Our children, all with families of their own now, are scattered all over the U.S. Los Vegas, Nevada and Queensland, Australia. It was always fun to visit with them and their families no matter how far we had to go.

Chapter 16

Vacationing in the Mountains

For many years we spent summer months at Yosemite National Park or Bass Lake with our family thanks to our friends Willard and Isabelle Ayers. We'd pack our gear and venture up the mountains with our five sons and one grandmother or the other, who both loved going with us. We could spend as much time as we wanted; in Yosemite, we'd stay anywhere from two weeks to a month.

The Yosemite Valley cabin, nestled beyond the Wawona Hotel, was isolated among the huge Sequoias but had some clear land where the boys could play. It had a fireplace, which separated the dining, and living rooms, two bedrooms, and one bath. Often there was no hot water or no running water at all. The boys needed daily baths, and sometimes we'd go to the river before dark—a shivering experience! It was a necessary evil, but the boys were good sports and made the best of it.

Other summers we'd venture to the Ayers' cabin in the vacation Town of Bass Lake. Willard taught me how to handle his boat, along with the rules and regulations of the lake. By this time all the boys were great swimmers, and I became chief pilot and engineer. The boys could fly down the river on water skis for as long as I could pilot the boat, and they never seemed to tire. I'm the one who got tired!

The town had a movie theater that Willard and Isabelle soon acquired. Boating by day and movies by night—what more could we ask? Their son operated the projector and their daughters ran the snack bar. Every summer was a joy to remember, and so much fun that we hated going home when our vacations ended. Jack had to work most of the time, although he made it a point to join us for a few days when ever it was possible for him.

The Ayers were a very enterprising family, yet were not the least bit selfish with their time or their worldly possessions, which they always shared freely and happily. We were ever so lucky and grateful to be blessed with such a wonderful family as our friends. Without their generous invitations we couldn't have afforded such special summer vacations. My mother and I would make it a point to do something special to the cabins in which we occupied. One year we painted the kitchen. It needed a new look. Will and Isabelle refused to charge us for our lengthy stay and it was our way of doing something special for them. I wanted to show our appreciation and this was a great way to help. They loved it.

Jack's mother, Doris, was so grateful for the Ayers' generosity that she painted a huge cypress mural for their Fresno home. It was beautiful, and we all celebrated its christening with a big dinner and a gathering of many friends. It was quite an occasion, and Grandma Doris was very proud and happy with herself. We were especially proud of her talent—she was in her late sixties at the time.

Early one morning in 1956, Isabelle called to say no one had spoken for their Yosemite cabin for the summer, and if we wanted to use it we were welcome to do so. I thanked her, and told her I'd talk to Jack and the boys about it, since school was still in session we had no plans as yet for summer vacation.

That evening at dinner I gave the boys options for summer vacation: go to the Fort for a couple of days, or to a couple of movies later in the summer, or go to Yosemite for a couple of weeks. Then I told them about Isabelle's call, and all the boys screamed with joy. They put their heads together, decided what they needed to take when the time came. They always packed their own cases. At times they'd ask my advice, but usually they did their thing without supervision.

Vacation time with so many children has its share of difficulties. Even with everything the boys would do to prepare for our vacation, plenty of work was left for me. Aside from the kitchen necessities, I had to consider medication and first aid, blankets and sleeping bags, and so on. After everybody and their belongings had been checked out, we'd say goodbye to Dad. He'd lecture the boys on what he expected of them during this trip. "Be attentive to mother and your grandmother, no fighting, and all that good stuff, OK." "Gotcha Dad." Was their eager and joyful reply?

My mother, Grandma, Alice Abeyta, would arrive a few days before our departure, packed and anxious to go. We packed the car and said a silent prayer for safety on the road, and away we went. The house was spotless the day we left; I was so proud of the way the boys had worked together and cleaned everything. As we were leaving, I thanked them for their work. Dennis was four then, and Jackie was nine.

After we'd arrived and unpacked, the boys changed into their swimming clothes and we headed straight for the river. Grandma stayed behind to clean the cabin and start our dinner. The boys loved the river so we went every day. It was fun time for them and it gave me a chance to sit and rest from the long trip. Since the water was so cold, all I did was dangle my feet in the river.

On one such excursion, I noticed Dennis was rather listless. He showed no interest in swimming and seemed irritated with the least little thing—strange and unusual behavior for him. I walked over to talk to him and as I did, I picked him up and realized that Dennis' whole body was as hot as a firecracker. Cold fear engulfed me. I told Jackie to get the boys together, that we were going back home. At the cabin Dennis' temperature was 102. I gave him baby aspirin and set him down to rest while Grandma and I got dinner; the boys changed their clothes and played quietly. After dinner Grandma helped them get ready for bed. We said our prayers and I kept Dennis with me during the night.

The next morning the fever was about the same. I drove to the Wawona Hotel and called Jack at the office. I explained the problem and we decided he needed to call our pediatrician about Dennis's fever and secure medication. I would then drive to Fresno for the medication while Grandma stayed with the boys. I took Terry with me for moral support and drove straight to the pharmacist, where the prescription awaited us. The doctor treated Dennis for Tonsillitis and we wasted no time in returning to the cabin. Dennis seemed to be feeling better, but still had a high temperature. I immediately started the medication, and in a couple of days he was almost back to normal, thank God—which we all did.

When I was sure he was out of danger, I thanked the boys for being so good while Dennis recuperated. I told them I felt he was too young to be romping in that ice-cold river. For the rest of that vacation I found other interests for him, and I was glad that he was so responsive and easy to entertain.

Originally, we had talked Jack into joining us at the cabin for the weekend before we left for Yosemite. We were all excited and did special things for him, including baking a cake. Dad came rolling up early Friday afternoon and we spent the rest of the day entertaining him. It was such a pleasure to have him with us even for just a couple of days.

The next morning Jack took us down to the Big Valley to check out all the programs there for the little guys, which included our boys. We had so much fun, and then he drove us through the enormous Sequoias—literally! A tree had been carved through at ground level to form a tunnel. Driving through it was a real treat. We parked got out of the car, and Jack carved "Nutter's Inc. Saturday August 1956" in the trunk of that tree. The boys were so excited, "Dad, look at all the different names carved in this tree. We are part of history. What a great feeling!" It was such a special day for all of us.

On Sunday morning, Dad took us to the top of the mountain. During the summer the park had a spectacular program on the mountain top plateau, which folks watched from below. They usually employed huge balls of falling fire cascading down into the valley. I'm not sure just how they did it, but it was a beautiful sight. Dad wanted to see where the events took place, so up the skinny road we drove. Today that program has been outlawed and is non-existent.

Arriving at the top we parked the car and discovered the plateau ended sharply with a sheer drop miles down into the valley. The only protection for viewers was a short pipe railing that marked the boundary; it wasn't much of a barrier. Well, our number-two son, Patrick, had no fear of anything. He ran toward that railing at full speed and dropped into a slide until his foot hit that rail, with a playful scream all the way to that pipe. I fell to the ground in complete panic, my body ice cold and shivering uncontrollably in terror. I scuttled backwards on the ground as I pleaded with Jack to collect the boys. Jackie grabbed Patrick as he made another run and pulled him back to where I was. "You're scaring Mother." All I said was, "Please, everybody in the car."

During the long drive down the hill, Jack tried to reassure me everything was A-OK, although he couldn't understand what was wrong. I told him and the boys I was sorry. They had no fear whatsoever and they really felt terrible for me. I couldn't wait to get back to the safety of the cabin. Grandma made dinner while Dad and the boys played chess. Jack would look at me and say occasionally, "Feel better?" I simply shook my head "Yes." As I rested I looked over my gang and said a silent prayer thanking God that nothing horrible had happened on top of that mountain. For years I've been fearful of heights, but I hid it within myself never admitting this fear to anyone. Just walking into an elevator was difficult for me. I never admitted any of this to my parents. What a rude awakening for them!

On Monday Jack was scheduled to return to Fresno, but he stayed for most of the day and played with the boys in the cabin. It was peaceful, and I truly had no desire to leave. When all was quiet, the deer would venture to their table in front of the dining room. Our friend Willard had made that table especially for all the animals. They would eat the food that we'd leave out for them. Their jaws made such a crunching sound when they ate that it sounded like their teeth were loose. It was so funny.

Before returning to Fresno, Jack had a long talk with the boys about their taking care of Grandma and Mom. The boys assured Dad that everything would be just fine while he was gone. Jackie added, "And we're not going to go to the top of that mountain again, are we, Mom?" "No," I said, "no way!" We all kissed Dad goodbye, walked him to his car, and waved until he disappeared down the road.

Grandma and I cleaned the kitchen while the boys played more chess and checkers. There was no television or radio, so we entertained ourselves in various ways until it was time to hit the sack. It wasn't until I told the boys to get ready for bed that I realized one of them was missing. I did a head count and realized Patrick wasn't there. I questioned the boys, and we looked in all the rooms, but he was nowhere to be found.

I decided to play Patrick's game of hide-and-seek. I told Grandma that, since it would be dark soon, I'd go outside and call to him just in case he was teasing us. When the boys played this game at home, if we called out a third time that meant we'd given up they'd won, and they would come in on their own. Well, I called him three times—and when he didn't appear, I panicked. For him to disappear at this time was all I needed.

I went back in the house and, as calmly as I could, told Grandma that I needed to call the park rangers and inform them about Pat. She wondered aloud, "Is it possible that Jack might have taken him?" Never, I said; Jack would tell me first. We were both frightened, so I questioned the boys again. They knew nothing. We then nervously tucked the boys in bed. I knew Jack would go to the office before he went home, and that he'd be there by now. I decided to put off calling the rangers until after I'd talked to Dad, so I drove down to use the Wawona Hotel's public telephone. The boys were safely in bed under my mother's watchful eye, so I took my time.

When Jack answered the phone I started out calmly enough, but soon I burst into tears and blurted out, "We can't find Patty. He's not here. Honey, did he by chance come home with you?" "Of course not," he said. "I wouldn't take him without telling you." I screamed with fear, as Jack did what he could to calm me. "He's so little and it's so cold in the night," I sobbed. "He'll freeze to death out there in that wilderness before we find him! What should I do? What should I do?" I fought to regain my composure and told Jack that I would call in the rangers.

"Just a minute," Jack said firmly. "I'll be right back." I waited in agony, and then a little voice came on the phone and said, "I'm sorry, Mommy." I was so relieved to hear Pat's voice the tears started again. I heard Dad say, "See what you're doing to Mommy! Aren't you ashamed of yourself?" In a tiny voice my son repeated, "I'm sorry, Mommy."

Jack took the phone and told me he'd found Patrick on the floor of the back seat, sound asleep. He'd had no idea our son was there. "You know now he's safe. Tell me, where you are calling from?" "I am at the Wawona Hotel." "If you hadn't gone straight to the office, I'm not sure what I would've done." He then told me to go back to the cabin and get some sleep. "You can pick Pat up here in the morning at your leisure. Please take your time and drive carefully." "OK honey, thanks."

The irony struck me as I drove back to the cabin: Patrick was the one who always got carsick. It amazed me that with Jack driving around those mountain curves he made the trip into the city with absolutely no problem. When I told grandma that Pat was safe, she gave a big sigh of relief. It is so easy in prayer to be thankful when everything turns out great.

When I think back to our little-boys years, I'm amazed by all that transpired between the six of us. Dad was always so busy working, yet he never objected to our busy activities. Best of all, he saw to it we had enough funds to do what we wanted. The Ayers were so gracious in allowing us to occupy their summer cabin, that alone is something we will never forget, but it was still a costly excursion.

What I didn't teach the boys, they taught me! As a matter of fact I found myself wondering about that from time to time. Even so, I certainly remained determined not to let them lose sight of who was the boss. We always knew that we could count on Dad's help and his word was final, if it ever came to that.

Those were busy happy years we can all look back on with such beautiful cherished memories.

Chapter 17

Membership Drives and Closet Incidents

*I*n 1956 Sacred Heart School held there annual bazaar, and I was asked to be chairman. (These days I'd be the "chairperson.") The honor included a lot of hard work, which started six months prior to the event itself. Coordinating all the different booths, the door prizes, and the raffle for a donated Cadillac coupe was almost too much for me, so my parents decided to come and help me with the final preparations.

The day before the event, my mother (Grandma Abeyta) and I collected all the door prizes that were promised by the different businesses in the community. As we were doing this, the booth chairmen were building their individual booths on the church grounds. Exhausted, Mother and I headed home, only to find a lot of action in front of our house. Two big fire trucks filled the front of our property. I parked and frantically ran to Jack and the little boys, who were hanging onto him.

When Jack saw me, he said "Don't worry, honey, everything is fine now." When I asked what he meant, he said, "Well, we had a little fire here." "A *little* fire!" I said, stricken. As I roamed the circumference of the property I saw my entire wardrobe strewn across the lawn, half burnt. My beautiful Lilly Ann suits, everything, gone. I fought for control while my mother held me with tears in her eyes. I kept asking myself how could this happen. My heart was beating like a drum, and my entire body shook uncontrollably. At one point I thought I'd collapse. Jack grabbed me as I was starring down at my half burnt clothes, he held me for a minute and said, "Please don't worry honey. All this is just material things and they can be replaced." I fought back the tears.

Gramps came over to me and said we were really lucky. They'd all been in the living room watching TV when Dad smelled smoke and asked Jackie to check all the rooms. Jackie returned and reported that my closet was on fire and immediately he ran for the hose outside our bedroom window. Gramps called the fire department. Dad stood at my closet door with the hose in hand, the fire blazing, and no water—the key to the faucet was missing. Finally Jackie got the water turned on and Dad managed to extinguish the fire before the firemen arrived. They checked the walls of the closet to make sure it was free from danger, and smeared cream on Dad's blistered hand. He had tried to save some of my clothes but the hangers were so hot he had to let go. His hand took weeks to heal and not once did he complain about the pain. It was nothing, he said, but I knew better and I ached for him. I knew his heart was aching for me.

Gramps and the boys had tried to save my clothes too, but everything was gone. The only wearable garments I had were on my back, and the next day was the bazaar. My car was loaded with door prizes and I needed to stay focused in order to get through the next two days. Having my mother and father there was a blessing.

It was an accident, but one that could easily have been prevented. Many months prior to this, we'd taken the boys to a horse show at the L.A. Coliseum. That evening the emcee announced that all lights would be extinguished, and on the count of three, everyone in the bleachers was to strike a match in the darkness. What a sensational sight that was! It deeply impressed our number-three son, Terry.

The day before the bazaar everyone was busy, and Terry was so bored he decided to recreate the scene again in my dark closet. When the boys were questioned about the fire, Terry's shoulders sagged. He looked up at Dad with tears in his eyes and casually admitted that he'd done it. When he was questioned as to, "Why" he found it difficult to explain. He hadn't intended to burn anything, and when my dress ignited as he struck the match, it frightened him. He ran out of the closet and shut the door behind him, hoping to smother the fire.

As upset as I was with Terry, one look at his face and my anger melted away. He couldn't look up at me, and I could see the fear and shame in his face. He felt so bad, and seemed depressed; such strong feelings for his young years. He knew he'd done something wrong and that bad consequences had come of it. He didn't need me to punish him any further. Nothing is going to bring back my wardrobe. It was a bitter lesson for him, and he never played with matches again. But I was devastated.

That evening as I lay in bed feeling sorry for myself, Jack came to me holding a pair of his shoes and said, "Honey, I'm putting these in your closet just so it doesn't get lonely tonight." I couldn't help but smile. I asked, "Honey, do you believe these boys will reach age twenty-one?" He held me close in his arms and said, "Of course they will, this is just another one of those experiences." "Yes honey, it's easy for you to say that, but look around you. The house smells terrible, and I have no idea what I'm going to wear to the bazaar tomorrow. God give me strength, is all I ask." I looked up and smiled at him again. He held me in his arms until I fell asleep. No matter how bad he felt he never let on to me. Instead he showed compassion for my feelings. Yet, I know he suffered a great deal within.

Mother and Dad helped me to get things going at the church while Jack took a couple hours off. That evening he presented me with a new outfit to wear for the next day. I was so elated with his thoughtfulness I simply hugged him and cried in his arms. To this day I cannot remember what he purchased; I just remember the outfit was perfect and beautiful. I could only say "Thank you honey over and over again." I had something new to wear to the bazaar on Sunday!!!

On the third day after all booths were broken down our pastor called a meeting to thank the committee for their dedicated work. We were given a track sheet of each booth, which indicated the total monies taken in during those two days. The raffle alone brought in $5,000; including the booths, we raised a grand total of over $8,000! Father cheerfully gave us his blessing and expressed his heartfelt thanks for a truly successful event.

I personally called a luncheon meeting for my committee. The goals we had set from day one had led to this success, and I wanted to express my thanks—not only to the women but also to their husbands for building the booths and tearing them down. God always allows us to work miracles when we set our minds to it. I got as far as saying "Thanks, everyone!" when one of the women stood up and presented me with a gift certificate from our local fabric store. It was no secret about our fire incident, and their thoughtfulness struck me speechless. All I could manage to say was "Thank you again." I wasted no time with that certificate and I made two skirts and a couple of blouses right away. Now I had three outfits in my lonely stinking closet.

The boys all started kindergarten at Chester Rowell and went on to Sacred Heart Grade School. After three years the diocese changed the school districts, and our street fell in the district of St. John's Catholic Grade School. Our older boys were transferred from Sacred Heart to St. Johns and Dennis came directly from Chester Rowell to St. John's. All five of the boys walked to and from St. John's every day. They were quite a sight, the whole pack of them making that five-mile trip—unheard of these days!

Dennis's first grade teacher, Sister Guadalupe called me one afternoon. She was concerned because, during recess, the girls were constantly running after our son and kissing him. In Sister's opinion Dennis was at fault, and she wanted me to put a stop to this. I assured her that I'd have a long talk with my number-five son, and that evening after dinner I confronted him with his teacher's accusation.

Dennis told me that he didn't cause the problem. "Mom, it embarrasses me when the girls stare at me and giggle, so I just get up and walk away. When I do, they run after me." I asked him about the kissing. He said he knew he could outrun the girls, but he didn't want to disappoint them, so he'd slow down—and when they caught him, they'd kiss him. Privately, I was amused, but I talked to him seriously about using discretion. I told him he'd have to ignore the girls and stop this kind of play. If Sister calls me about this again I'm not going to be very happy. It has got to stop. "Do you understand, Dennis?" "I guess." "Really Dennis, this is serious." "Yes, I know. It will not happen again Mom." "I understand your position, but it is best if you just keep active with the boys in your class. Then the girls won't be tempted." "Ok Mom."

I was asked to join the school's Mothers' Club. The club helped the pastor raise money for school expenses, and there seemed to be a great deal of them! We paid club dues and held fundraising events at different times of the year, including bake sales, carni-

120

vals, and raffles. Our pastor was always there to push. I worked in every aspect of the club. The only office I declined was that of Treasurer; the responsibility for money outside my own household was out of the question for me.

One day the club president asked me to accept the responsibility of Membership Chairman, encouraging mothers to join the club and collecting yearly dues. I asked myself, where do I start? After dinner I conferred with my sons about this, and asked their opinion.

Jackie said, "Mom, you're asking mothers to join the club when they're busy with their own families." "Yes, and so am I." Jackie continued, "Most of them feel that their obligation ends when they pay for their children's education here at St. Johns." "Oh, great," I said wryly. "What are you trying to tell me?" "Do you think you can involve the different classes along with the students in those classes? Each of the boys said, sure Mom, that's the way to do it. You need to give the kids some incentive, that way they will become part of the program. That's a great idea Jack. But I wonder how? "You'll come up with something Mom!" "Ok, honey, I'll give it some serious thought."

In a short letter I appealed to all the mothers about our membership drive, which was to take place the following month. I explained that we needed to collect yearly dues of only $1.00 per household and mapped out where the money went when we collected it. I thanked them for their consideration and cooperation. This letter was sent home with every child in the school. Surely $1.00 a year was nothing. Some families had three to six children in attendance.

I bought eight 36"x36" white art boards to implement my plan of action. Every class needed to have its own chart. I appealed to my artist friend Margie Rodgers to do a special art design for each class. As I dictated she drew what I wanted. It was so much fun.

The first grade chart showed Humpty Dumpy on a brick wall. The wall comprised just the right amount of bricks for that class. As the children brought in their membership dollars, they each colored in a brick and added their name to it. The class was thrilled with it.

The second grade chart had Snow White sitting on the edge of a pond. Each child in the class received a cutout of a little white duck when they brought in their dues. The little girls were especially clever as they drew little dresses on the ducks, initialed them, and placed them wherever they wanted on the lake. The whole class loved their chart.

The third grade chart featured Nancy of the funnies. Freckles were added to her face. When the children were through with Nancy, she was hilarious. She had freckles in her ears and eyebrows and on the tip of her nose.

The other grades' art boards were just as charming. Seventh grade had a baseball player standing at home plate ready to swing. The children stuck their baseballs all over the board. Eighth grade had a football star kicking high in the air, and the footballs flowed off the chart and on to the blackboard. It was so funny and fun for all.

There wasn't a child in the school who didn't participate. We achieved 100% membership and were complimented many times over. We also had better attendance for our holiday bake sales and other events when they rolled around. My sons would beam with pride about all that was done to achieve a successful drive. They were proud of me, and it was because of them that I maintained a concentrated effort.

The year sped by quickly; all the activity of our home and the additional lessons for the boys kept me busy. The boys never neglected their daily duties, and I remained mindful of my throat problem and took care of my health. Five months on my back had made me a different individual.

Much to my dismay, the following year I was elected Membership Chairman again. I tried to get someone else to accept the responsibility with my assistance, but unfortunately no one had the inclination. What could I do this year without repeating? Again I went to my sons, but no one could give me a clue. Dennis said, "Pray for this one, Mom, and I know you'll come up with something." 'Thanks fellows." I was checking the calendar, circling the monthly holidays, when a brainstorm hit me.

I wrote another letter announcing that the yearly drive would commence the following month. I concentrated on Halloween, which was coming up. I outlined my plan to my friend Margie and asked her to draw a large pumpkin on an 8½"x11" sheet of paper. I printed enough copies for the whole school. There were no class charts this time; each child received a paper pumpkin to color and take home. Both the letter and the pumpkin were sent home that same day. A few days passed and the dollar bills started to roll in and we all jumped for joy, we were so thrilled.

In November, Margie drew a wonderful Pilgrim. Over his shoulders she created the saddest and skinniest turkey you ever saw, with stars in his eyes. He was priceless. The children laughed and commented about him for the longest time. Our November bulletin was popular among all the students.

Margie's artwork for December was a graceful depiction of the Nativity, and it was precious. Jesus' Mother Mary's face was lovely, and the girls in the class used color crayons and made her garments and her face even more beautiful. My monthly bulletins kept reminding parents to pay their club dues, and before we knew it we had another 100% success with our drive. Our pastor was ever so happy, and thanked the club with a gracious letter to every member in the school. It seems that my work at school was ever constant.

The boys loved to wrestle with Dad, but it played havoc with the furniture. One Sunday afternoon they were so loud and reckless with each other, banging the chairs with their feet and bodies that I yelled at them to stop. I was ignored. I could take it just so long, and then I ventured into the kitchen and filled a big glass with cold water. I yelled again, and when they ignored me I threw the cold water on both Jack and Jackie, and then ran with all my might. Dad yelled to the boys, "Don't let Mother get away, grab her!"

But I got away and hid in the very small linen closet across from the bathroom. The space between the shelves was only fifteen inches apart. When I closed the door I knew I was there to stay because that door couldn't be opened from the inside. I felt certain I'd be found and have to take the consequences for the cold water. Well, no matter.

Everybody looked for me except Jack. The minutes dragged by, and soon I realized they were tired of searching. I could hear Jack as he questioned his sons, going over all the possible hiding places in the house. "Are you sure you looked here? How about there?" Jackie replied, "I can't imagine where Mom went. I even looked in both cars." Dad said, "Oh well, she'll come back soon."

Meanwhile, I had become really cramped in that small space, and the air was getting thin. I began to feel a little nervous. I thought if I don't let them know I'm in here, and they go outside, I wouldn't have a snowball's chance of getting out of here. Then I heard Jack say, "Let's all get dressed and surprise Mom when she returns. Then we'll take her out to dinner." I could hear him shaving in the bathroom, and could hear the boys as they sat on the sink, watching and talking to him. I was furious; I thought I'd suffocate in there if I didn't do something quick. I knocked on the door to let them know where I was.

"Somebody please see who's at the front door," Dad said. Michael ran back and said, "Nobody." "That's strange," Front door, I said to myself, can't they detect the knock is coming from this closet door? I knocked again, this time really hard. I heard some shuffling of shoes on the floor and slowly the door opened. Jack had the razor in his hand with his face half shaven. All the boys screamed with laughter. "Look at Mom, she looks like a sardine!" "Help me," I said, and Dad reached in to pull me out with one hand, saying, "I can't believe you fit in there." "I can't believe it either," I gasped. It took some time to unfold my legs and get my circulation going again. Everybody felt so sorry for me. They tried to talk to me as I tried to straighten my limbs, but they were laughing too hard. Patrick said, "Mom, you looked so funny in there!" "Right. Thanks for finding me, fellows." Michael asked, "How did you get in there so fast?" Sarcastically I said, "I took a plane." The laughter from all of them was something else. I didn't mention the cold water; I let them feel sorry for me instead. They said that they were thinking of taking me out to dinner to my favorite restaurant. "Yes, I heard you," I said. "Do you suppose we can take in a movie too?" Jack said, "Sure, why not? It's your day, Mom." I was very proud of myself. Getting a dinner and a movie too—how special! Usually I didn't get such royal treatment when I was in trouble. Getting Dad to a movie is really special. To him that is a waste of time.

Can you imagine, all of us together for one full evening what a real treat? The boys were always so well behaved and so well mannered it was a pleasure taking them to dinner. Dad's time was so consumed with work that it was very special when he would make time to be with us, even if only on a Saturday or a Sunday.

It is difficult for him to understand our need of him. We are taken for granted so much of the time, but for me I'll take any day of the week to have him with us. That's not a sacrifice, that is what you call LOVE.

Chapter 18

Inspiration, Pro and Con

*O*ur dear friends Ed and Marjorie Rodgers were an inspiration to us. Ed worked for Jack for many years and he had a dream: More than anything in the world he wanted a swimming pool in his own yard. He didn't enjoy going to the beach or a public pool. He and Margie decided that, since they had enough space in their back yard, they were going to have their own pool.

They measured the size and depth of an average-size pool and dug the hole with the aid of some machinery. As the dirt was coming up and out, Margie would wheelbarrow the dirt to different sections of the property for flowerbeds. I'm not sure how long it took to reach its final stages, but the both of them became more and more excited as the day neared. Once their portion of the digging was finalized, a professional company poured the foundation. Before long the pool was finished and ready for use—new, clean and beautiful.

We received a formal invitation to join the Rodgers on the occasion of their first party with this new pool. It was a priceless invitation that Margie, a professional commercial artist, drew up herself. I passed it around to the boys and asked if they wanted to join the Rodgers in their new pool. "What a silly question," they answered. "OK." In that case I'm going shopping for new swimsuits for you boys. Everything is new over at the Rodgers', so let's not disappoint them by our appearance. With new shirts, swim trunks, and extra large towels for each boy, we were ready.

The day before the party, Dad and I reviewed the rules and regulations of pool activity to the boys. "Fort Washington rules apply at the Rodgers'; the only difference is that we're in a private residence. Should there be any activity that is not allowed, you will sit on the bench. Understood?" The boys nodded.

When we arrived the boys greeted the Rodgers, thanked them for inviting us, and complimented them on their beautiful pool. They looked it over and its surroundings, and were so tickled they could hardly wait to jump in the water. Terry called out to Ed, "Is it OK if we go into the pool now, Mr. Rodgers?" Ed called back to the boys, "It's OK, guys, but not before you read the Rules of the Pool. They're posted by the cabana." The boys walked over to the cabana and Terry dramatically read the rules aloud:

RULES OF THE POOL

1. There will be no yelling in the Pool.
2. There will be no rough stuff in the Pool.
3. There will be no running in the Pool Area.
4. There will be no sharp objects thrown in the Pool.
5. There will be no peeing in the Pool.

By Manager and Owner: Ed Rodgers

All of the boys chuckled at the last rule, and then Terry turned around and said, "Gotcha, Mr. Rodgers," as he made the OK sign. "OK, go for it!" said Ed—and from there on out it was play, play, play. The invitations never stopped.

Margie and I agreed that after the pool exercise lunch should be served in the cabana. Ed was master at the barbecue, so they'd serve the main course and I'd bring the rest of the goodies. One time I made a large green salad with all the trimmings, using small cherry tomatoes instead of chopped big ones. I served some to each one of the boys while they waited for Ed to serve the chicken, and when Ed asked for the salad, Terry piped up, "The salad is great, Mr. Rodgers, but be careful with those strawberries, they're terrible!" I said to Terry, "Cherry tomatoes honey." "Oh, he said sorry Mr. Rodgers."

On the side of their property the Rodgers had a spruce tree that stood taller than their two-story house. One particular Saturday afternoon, Jack and I decided to visit with Ed and Margie indoors before joining the boys at the pool. Shortly, way off in the distance, we heard a very soft voice saying in a long fashion "Hello, down there." After the third call, we all went outside to check it out. We then heard the same distant voice saying out loud dragging his voice in a long fashion. "U p p p h e r e!" Jackie rushed over to Dad and said, "Look where Pat is!" as he pointed to the top of that spruce tree. We were astounded as to how high he was.

Pat had one leg and one arm wrapped around the very tip of that tree. It was new growth and very thin, and Pat was swaying back and forth. Ed was terribly nervous. He said over and over again, "Don't get excited anyone, and please don't get excited!" Margie and I stood still, holding our breath. Finally Jack was able to speak, he said as softly as he could with both hands cupping his mouth, "That's great, son. Ed has some ice cream for you, so come on down." We heard him say "OK," loud and long again, as we watched him climb back down. I could see the anger mounting in Jack's face; Pat had really scared him again.

When Pat was down and said "OK Dad, where's the ice cream?" Jack said, "I told you a big white lie. There's no ice cream for you because you don't deserve it. Get it?" His tone was harsh and very stern. "The very idea you're going up that tree, you could have broken that beautiful top. How could you take that chance? You owe Mr. Rodgers an apology." Bowing his head saying, *"I'm sorry, Mr. Rodgers."* "That's OK, Pat; just see to it that you never do that again." *"I won't, sir."* And he never did. Pat was such a dare devil and too young in years to understand the consequences of some of the things he did. He kept me on pins and needles so much of the time.

After dinner one evening Jack asked me to call Mrs. S. to come over for an hour. He and Ed had unfinished business at the office and they needed to talk. Our sitter was not at home so it was impossible for me to leave. He insisted that the boys were old enough surely they could manage with out Mom for an hour. Jackie assured us they would be fine, so I went with Dad. About twenty-five minutes later Mike appeared at the Rodgers front door. He was frantic and said there had been a bad accident. We rushed home to find that Jackie had Dennis lying on the sink in the bathroom cleaning a long gash over his right eye. Mike had grabbed Dennis in the back yard and swung him in a circle, suddenly releasing him as his body flew forward and his forehead hit the redwood bench. We had to rush Dennis to Emergency as Dennis continued to apologize to us for the problem. Jack was furious with the attending physician. Dennis must have been his first eye case. We were extremely nervous as we watched the Doctor proceed to close the gash above his eyebrow with a curvature needle but his hand could not stop shaking. Dad was so angry he wanted to call in another doctor. After that incident I never allowed Jack to talk me into leaving the boys alone again.

For the Fresno Centennial, the news media announced that all the men in town were expected to sprout either a beard or a mustache for the festivities. On the day of the Centennial, some sort of penalty would be imposed on clean-shaven males. They hadn't decided just what sort of penalty at that point, but plans were in the making. The penalty was kept under raps until the big day.

I bought the boys special checkered shirts for the occasion. They each wore a different pastel color: yellow, blue, green, pink, and orange. Ironically, the boys complained about going to school because they didn't have beards. Imitation beards or mustaches were being sold, but there had to be a better way. When I asked Dennis whether he wanted a beard or a mustache, he replied, "Both!" So, using an eyebrow pencil, Grandma Doris and I drew a handsome mustache that curled at the ends, and then added a short beard. Dennis looked in the mirror and thought he was so handsome. Each boy sported the same and our friend Ed Rodgers took a group picture of them. The boys marched to school with pride and everybody admired their ingenuity.

For Christmas 1958 Jack felt that the boys should have bikes. I said Dennis and Michael were too young, and suggested he get three bikes for the older boys. He disagreed, we discussed it, and I relented. "OK, but if anything goes wrong, you'll have to accept the responsibility. I still think they're too young." But Jack had confidence in his boys. "What can go wrong?" he said.

Christmas morning was glorious. Everybody was happy with their new bikes. On their first ride Dad tested each bike; it took some time for Dennis to get started, but Michael did great. The other boys were a cinch to ride with no problem. Dad set up very strict rules for all five boys to abide by or else lose their biking privileges.

The first week the boys were allowed to go around the block. Unknown to us, construction workers had left a large pile of dirt in the middle of the block behind our street. All of the boys decided to take a flying leap over it on their bikes, not knowing there was a huge hole in the ground beside it. Jackie went first, and everybody made it fine except Dennis. His bike landed in the hole and he tore his cheek on his flashlight holder. A neighbor brought him home and told me what had happened. I thanked the neighbor and turned my attention to my injured son.

The blood running down his cheek frightened me, but since Dennis was crying so hard he needed attention. I cleaned the wound, and he cried off and on while I held him in my arms. The incident frightened him and he promised he'd never do that again. His cheek hurt, and his bicycle wheel was bent. I am sure the bent wheel on his bicycle worried him. It was a good lesson and, it made him think about venturing into something without first investigating. The four boys really felt bad and apologized to Dennis for leading him into danger without caution.

When Dad came home that night, he realized I was upset the moment he walked in the door. When we told him what had happened that day, it really angered him. He blamed the older boys for leading Dennis in to danger. We spent a great deal of time that evening discussing the incident. The boys promised Dad that they'd use more discretion in the future. Dad checked Dennis's scared cheek and told him that he needed to be especially careful in areas that are new to him. Dennis understood and apologized for causing such a fuss.

It was later this same year when Jackie and Pat wanted to have a paper route. Dad gave it some thought and agreed to help them get started. They loved The Fresno Bee and eagerly folded and delivered their papers to their assigned customers. Their take home pay was very small, but it was really appreciated.

About this time I decided we needed to reorganize ourselves. The boys' bedroom was overflowing with clothes and toys and school supplies, and it was becoming harder all the time for them to get their homework done. So we cleared out the garage (that had been converted into an office for Jack originally) and converted it into both a bedroom for Jackie and Patrick plus a study hall for all the boys. We set up bookshelves, work areas, and purchased five desks and chairs. Each boy's name was inscribed on a plaque attached to his own desk. They loved that, especially Jackie, whose plaque read "Jack Jr." (I had specifically ordered "Jackie.") I was upset about it until number-one son told me it was perfect, because he was so proud to *be Jack Jr.*—and that he was too old to be called Jackie anymore! Nevertheless, that change took some time for me to adjust. It was too easy for me to say "Jackie."

Dad was notoriously bad about shopping for himself, so I bought all his clothes: trousers, suits, shirts, ties, shoes, and the like. When a holiday rolled around I always went to Harry Coffee's, my favorite men's store, and bought something for each one of the boys to give to Dad. I'd take the gifts home and wrap them, allowing each boy to see what they were giving their father for his birthday, or whatever holiday was on deck. This went on for many years, and the salesman who always waited on me, Mr. Pulaski, eventually asked me when I was going to bring the little guys in to meet him.

I gave it some thought and before Father's Day in 1959 I told the boys it was time they went shopping with me for Dad. They were old enough and knew his likes and dislikes. They were excited and thought that it was a great idea. For our shopping spree the boys were dressed in their best look-alike clothes and we all piled into the car and headed for Harry Coffee's. Mr. Pulaski was elated when we appeared at the store's entrance. He greeted me with "Good afternoon, Mrs. Nutter," and continued nonstop about my previous shopping trips for gifts for the boys to give to their father. He was so excited he was positively gushing.

The boys glanced over to me, a bit overwhelmed. Before I could say a word, number-three son Terry took three steps backward, folded his arms across his chest, and said, "I've never seen this lady before in my entire life!" With that the other boys did the same. Mr. Pulaski laughed so hard his face turned as red as beet.

I appealed to these misfit jokers of mine, and after a few seconds Jack walked over to Mr. Pulaski, extended his hand, and stated he was the oldest. All the boys did likewise in turn. They were such gentlemen that the entire men's department staff wanted to wait on them. Afterwards we went to our favorite restaurant for lunch, loaded with an abundance of Father's Day gifts. The boys had a ball discussing their experience with Mr. Pulaski. From that day on the boys shopped for their father's gifts as all the holidays rolled around. What a teat for me.

Almost all the boys' clothes came from Coffee's. Mrs. Chamberlin in the boys department always informed me when a new shipment of T-Shirts came in. She would pick five shirts alike and call me. Their Fashion Show for the younger boys and girls took place in the summer. One year when Dennis was five she asked me if she could feature him in their Fashion Show. Dennis was delighted and I told him as he walked down the ramp, he could throw me a kiss. He not only threw me a kiss, but with both hands he threw kisses to the whole crowd. He was a sweetheart and everybody really loved him.

Yours truly frequented Harry Coffee's beautiful ladies department regularly many times over the years. One year long before Christmas Mrs. Lacy (the sales lady who always waited on me in her department) found me admiring a beautiful handbag. It was beige in color, hard plastic with different bright decorative sequences. She took the liberty of calling Jack at his office telling him about my visit. With Christmas around the corner she said, "You might want to surprise your wife with this really special purse." He politely said, "Mrs. Lacy, I would like to get my *Thanks Giving Turkey Dinner Down* before shopping for Christmas." She was embarrassed and apologized. Christmas morning the boys found a beautifully wrapped package under the tree with a tag saying, To Mom from Dad with Love. What I saw really made me wonder! "Thanks honey it's beautiful." Jack then told me the story and how he came to make this purchase. I apologized for Mr. Lacy and I thanked him for taking the time to check this purse out. At this writing it was forty six (46) years ago. It is one of the only bags that I have kept over the years and it is still beautiful. Occasionally I use it today.

No matter where the boys would go, our sons were known as the very polite Nutter boys. Pat and Terry were only a year apart and about the same height; neither went anywhere without the other, and they were nearly always asked if they were twins. Well, Terry soon tired of this. Once when a Mothers' Club member who said, "Oh, you're the Nutter boys," Terry immediately answered, "Yes, we are, thank you—and no, we're not twins!" Later that member called me to inform me of the incident. She said she was very impressed with the boys. She asked me several questions about each of the boys. I answered as best as I could but in my mind I was, without a doubt very proud of our sons. Terry was so young but he seemed to have a capacity to read peoples minds and acted accordingly. He was so much like his Dad.

Fresno, California Centennial Celebration
100th Anniversary
Not a clean face was seen on that day
Jack was No Exception.
He was called "Honest Abe."

These boys would not go to school for the
Celebration until they sported their fancy
"𝕭eards and 𝕸ustache's."
From Left to Right
𝕻atrick, 𝕸ichael, 𝕿erry and 𝕯ennis

Chapter 19

Moving to the Palos Verdes Peninsula

*I*n September 1960 Jack announced to me that another major move was imminent. His company known as "Cigarette Service Company of Fresno" was about to become a subsidiary of the parent company in Culver City. He is to become one of the vice presidents currently known as ARA (Automatic Retailers of America.) meaning a need for us to leave Fresno. His eyes sparkled with excitement!

Nothing of this nature was ever a problem for me; my love for my husband comes first, before any concerns about where we lived. To me, my responsibility was to support him and our sons. Wherever he needed to go we needed to follow.

As he spoke I couldn't help but think of the boys. By this time our two oldest sons were almost teenagers, who had acquired friends here and their personal lives were rooted in Fresno. They were very settled in their lifestyle. I felt the necessity of informing them personally of this up-coming change. I told Jack we should give the boys a chance to express themselves, and he agreed. "You're the boss, Mom. But remember, there's a lot at stake here!"

The next day I told the boys I was planning a special dinner for Saturday evening, and before I could continue Patrick asked, "We get to eat in the dining room, Mom?" "Right," I answered. "Dinner will be served at six. I want you boys to be ready?" They looked at each other questioningly, and then Jack Jr. said, "All we want to know, Mom, is everything OK?" I gave them a big grin and said everything was fine. "OK, then, we'll be ready." But as they walked away they muttered, "Wonder what it's all about this time?"

Everybody was spic and span by six o'clock, including Mrs. Syvertsen, who had helped me prepare dinner again. As usual, Jack graciously said a special prayer before the meal and we all ate without a word. Just before dessert, I broke the silence. "OK, Dad, it's your turn this time. What's on your mind?" "Thanks Mom."

Jack spoke slowly. "As I look around this table, I realize my family is growing by leaps and bounds. And a pretty good-looking lot, I might add! Please know, fellows, the courtesy and respect you have shown to this community, and the respect and love you've had for each other over the years, has been a tremendous joy to me. You have achieved for all of us a most unique and outstanding family with an excellent reputation. I've been complimented on your behavior so many times over the years. It's meant a great deal to me, to Mom, and we're very proud of all of you. She's trained you well, and you've responded with respect." He swallowed several times and adjusted his seat and then his tie. Number-one son Jack filled in the silence. "We love you too, Dad, and we're proud of you."

"Thanks, Jack, I think I needed that. OK, guys, this is it in a nutshell. I've had many conversations with the home office in Culver City about transactions that are taking place within this company. It now seems likely that our company here in Fresno is going to be sold to a considerably larger firm; as a result, all of us here will become a part of what is called a subsidiary. In short, fellows, we're being asked to leave Fresno, and move on to a more convenient home office location. I trust I make myself clear." He scanned the boys' faces.

There was a long silence as the boys exchanged glances, and then Dad continued. "This is a great opportunity for all of us. My salary increase will not only help us now, but will also help us prepare for the cost of college tuition, as you boys reach college age. Please understand; it's because of the role I've played in helping this company reach the size it is today and for that reason I'm being considered for this new position after the larger firm acquires our business. Do you realize what a plus this is for all of us? I could go into more detailed explanation, but the point at this moment is, how do you boys feel about our relocating?" Silence befell the room! "I realize this is a sudden decision, and it's an inconvenient time of the year, as far as school is concerned, but are you boys with me? Do you think that we can make this work for the good of all? I don't want to leave Fresno without you!"

Dad looked at each silent boy in turn. "Let me ask you a question fellows. Would you rather be a little frog in a little pond, or a big frog in a big pond? Growth is a part of life! You've grown from kindergarten to high school. How do you suppose you got there? Sitting still? Do you get the picture?" No one said a word.

I broke the silence again. "I know where I want to be, and that's with you, Dad, no matter where you go." Then Terry spoke up. "I don't know about you guys," he said as he looked around the table, "but I'm not leaving Fresno, and if you make me leave, Dad, I'm not going to be very cooperative." I felt that he was being disrespectful to his father, but it was good that he spoke up. His feelings did count. Dad was none too pleased at the boys' lack of enthusiasm. Jackie said, "I don't think it's going to be too bad, fellows, as long as we don't have to live in Los Angeles."

At that point I asked Mrs. Syvertsen to serve her delicious dessert. After she left the table the only sound was the occasional creak of the floorboards when someone shifted nervously in their chair. The pause seemed to go on forever, but finally Dad broke the silence. In a careful but forceful voice he said, "This is not the end of the world, fellows." The boys remained quiet, apparently pondering the situation. Ultimately, we had no choice; we were going. After dessert Dad said, "Well, so long, fellows, it's been nice knowing you." My heart sank!

There was no doubt in my mind that the move was going to take place. We did our thing and gave the boys a chance to give this some serious thought. Regardless, they were going to have to accept it. There wasn't much time to think, as I knew that Dad had already accepted the position in Culver City. I assured him that I would personally talk to the boys at a more convenient time. They need time to think. Dad left the following Monday to settle himself in his new position and to search for another place to live. Pray tell, where to next? This residence in Fresno has lasted for eleven long years.

Jack decided that the Palos Verde's Peninsula would be an ideal place to live. He established himself at the home office in Culver City while a realtor lined up places for him to see after work. He picked out a house high on top of a hill in a gated community called Rolling Hills Estates. Once he decided on the location and the house, he called me.

"Honey, I think I found a house you're going to love. It's on the Palos Verde's Peninsula and has a terrific view. Call the airlines, fly to Los Angeles, and I'll pick you up at the airport and take you over to the property to check it out. If you like it, we'll start a thirty-day escrow." "Thirty days!" I said. "Wow, let's not let any grass grow under our feet." Jack was so excited that I did what he asked. I told the boys about his call and said I was leaving for Los Angeles in the morning. The boys still were less than enthusiastic, but at least they were cooperative. Even Terry seemed resigned. "If that's what we have to do, I guess that's it," was his response. At this time I really did not worry too much about him. I'll worry about him later.

Jack was waiting for me at the airport. We drove out to Rolling Hills, but he couldn't find the house. He finally called the realtor for directions, and moments later we drove into the circle driveway. The house was so big I couldn't imagine how I'd ever furnish it. Dad said that the only furniture he wanted me to bring was our bed, our new refrigerator, refinished dinning room set, and TV. Aside from linens and dishes, that was it. As I looked around the interior of this house, I couldn't help but think about that little house in Fresno. It would've been great to raise our boys in a house such as this when they were in their growing stages. Yet we were all happy in Fresno so what more could I ask! Jack said "How about it honey, you like it?" I shook my head "Yes" as I hugged him and took a last minute look around. He said, "You're going to love living up here. It is so beautiful especially at night." I felt like I was dreaming until he said I was to go home, sell the furniture, pack, and put the house up for sale. "My heart aches honey." "Why?" "This is going to be hard on the boys." "Don't worry honey; they are going to love it up here. They are going to have to understand that, this is our home now. Fresno is of the past." "OK." "I understand so lets keep our fingers crossed."

Jack called the realtor told him we were accepting the house, submitted the 20% down payment, and asked for a thirty-day escrow. The purchase price $79,000.00 no loan required. At the close of escrow the house was paid for in full. Jack had achieved a dramatic financial gain upon the sale of Cigarette Service Company of Fresno, which made the purchase of the Rolling Hills property a reality. It was a dream come true. He naturally felt a great deal of pride in his accomplishment, and now with this dream house, what more could we possibly want. How he loved this house, and how we loved him for it!

Returning to Fresno filled my heart with great sadness. Our lives were built around this community, and now I wasn't too sure I wanted to leave either. But far be it from me to tell the boys my true feelings; I had to treat this move the same as when we first left Los Angeles. I conferred with the boys that evening and they were still a little apprehensive, but they accepted it. I left it to them to inform their friends of our plans, give them our new address, and extend invitations to come see us at any time. They were to do their own packing. "Take what you're going to need, and leave the rest here." Mrs. Syvertsen helped me pack our dishes and the like. I called a realtor to list our home and made plans to leave in thirty days as per dad's request.

One month later, we all piled into the car with our precious little dog Lady and headed for Rolling Hills. As we backed out of the driveway, we all noticed Mrs. Syvertsen standing in the doorway crying. She was such a dear, and such an important part of our family, so Dad stopped the car. We all piled out again to hug her, tell her we loved her and to visit us any time she missed us. I told her that, just as soon as I finished furnishing the new house, I'd send her plane fare and she could visit us at her convenience. We left her with the sale of the house, and the remaining furniture to do with as she wished. Our previous neighbors later told us she missed us so much that she had no energy to do anything. We all made a special effort to visit her from time to time, and brought mementos that we'd made for her ourselves, which really pleased her. But she was not the same.

Lady slept on the floor of the car until we felt it was time for her to do her business. Dad stopped where there was plenty of room for her to express herself. I would call her then walk far away from the car and she'd follow, never taking her eyes off the car or me. She'd do her thing, run back to the car, jump in, and waited for us to return. She hadn't forgotten her previous experience and she didn't want to be left again. Lady was a special dog sent to us by God, and we were privileged to have her. How we all loved that little dog.

When we arrived in Rolling Hills our property was still in escrow, so we had to stay in a motel. *Sound familiar?* This presented a problem for us because dogs were not allowed in motels. The boys managed to smuggle Lady in and we cautioned her not to bark. Thinking back, it really amazes me how quiet Lady was. If something excited her, or if she heard strange footsteps, she only stood up on all fours, her head and eyes rolling around to each of us as if to ask, "May I bark?" All we had to do was shake our heads no, and she wouldn't utter a sound. When she needed to go outside, she'd run to the door and wag her tail until one of the boys carried her out. No one ever knew we had a dog in our room. We've had many dogs, but never one like her. Lady was 15 years old when she was killed by a passing car in front of our home. We buried her in her favorite site on the Rolling Hills property. Her death affected me more than the boys. After that I found it difficult to accept another animal in our home. It was many years before I even looked at another dog.

Once again we lived in a motel, but this time it was fun. We ate out for every meal and the boys could go swimming as much as they wanted. They loved motel living, which we did for only a week this time. If the boys were spoiled before, they were even more so with this move, but it was good for Dad and me to have this leisure time with them.

While we stayed at the motel, the boys acquired a map of Rolling Hills, known as the "City within a City" since it was a part of Palos Verde's. The map helped them become familiar with the details of this luxurious gated Community, and it wasn't long before they fell in love with the area and its surroundings. What a delight for me.

Patrick and Terry 1968
Rolling Hills High Parking Lot

Jackie on Leave from Electronics "A" School Treasure Island, Ca. 1968

Caballeros
Del Rancho
Rolling Rink
Rolling Hills,
California

Jack just back from
Showing
Bowe at Caballeras
Taken in front of 6
Chesterfield Road

Chapter 20

Settling into Our New Life

*I*n November 1960 just before Thanksgiving day we left the motel and headed up Palos Verde's Drive East. Four guarded gates, providing a sense of security for all residents, protected Rolling Hills. Shortly after we arrived at 6 Chesterfield Road, Lyons Van and Storage drove up with our belongings. What little furniture we had was set in their respective rooms in this beautiful new home.

And what a home it was! It encompassed 4600 square feet of floor space. We had a spectacular 180-degree view up the coast to Santa Monica, around to Los Angeles, and down and around to San Pedro. In the evening all the lights around us glistened in living color, and it was even more beautiful than one could imagine.

Just ahead of our circle driveway was a three-car garage. We had a large electric kitchen with space for a dinette set, a dining room, a large living room with a fireplace at the far end of the room, a laundry room, and three full baths! There were four bedrooms, a music room, which we used as our office, a family room—in which we could have parked six automobiles and still had plenty of extra room! Featuring a formal bar and a fireplace with a built-in barbecue on the side. Entertaining guests was a delight with this barbecue, a luxury we did not have in Fresno. On the east corner of the family room was a considerable size storeroom, which became our catch all room.

After the move to Rolling Hills had taken place Jack announced to me that the company now Automatic Retailers of America had presented a gift to Jack in the amount of $28,500.00 and a gift to Rachel in the amount of $28,500.00 along with 110 shares of stock to each of the five boys. This would make the total for $90,000.00 but based on that day's stock value it had hiked to $92,200.00.

The gifts of stock to the boys would be by direct transfer of stock for each of them with the inscription, "Jack W. Nutter and Rachel Nutter jointly or the survivor of them as the custodians for and under the California Uniform Gifts to Minors Act." The shares would be transferred directly to the boy's in their name, as each became 21.

Additionally in 1962 there was a cash gift of $12,000.00 to Jack and $12,000.00 to Rachel.

Again in 1963 there was another cash gift of $12,000.00 to Jack and another $12,000.00 to Rachel.

All gifts would be paid one-half by Davre Davidson and one-half by Henry Davidson. The gift tax would to be paid by Dave and Henry, both federal and state. It was *all gift stock* generated to the seven of us by Jack's employers in appreciation of Jack's devotion to the company over the years. The ARA stock Certificates were beautiful and they continued to grow which increased the value of the gifts. This generated a meaningful savings to the both of us that allowed security for the future.

No need for concern, as far as, college tuition for the boys. Jack's increase in salary at that time made life easy and meaningful. Such consideration from two *endearing employees* is hardly ever heard of today. To express our words of thanks for their generosity was hardly enough. It is certain there was a great deal of sacrifices over the years in order for Jack to succeed in this business but our love for each other made it possible and worthwhile. Both Davre and Henry recognized this and acted accordingly. We shall be eternally grateful.

To continue with the house, we proceeded to visit various furniture manufactures that could transform our ideas about the sofas we needed for this house into reality. We picked out a company who had a gigantic show room that was quite impressive. Their certified designer drew on paper, the style we suggested indicating the length and height of the proposed sofas. They had an array of sample materials to choose from and we picked the fabric we wanted them to use for each sofa. I always love doing things like this.

The designer came up with three different sofas to our liking and told us that they would be ready for delivery in six to eight months. During that time I had the interior of the house painted. I searched for new specially decorated *see through* chenille window coverings for the family room and living room. We picked out new white tile flooring for the kitchen, white curtains with lavender accents and a new electric stove top and hood.

The first contemporary sofa was for the *large family room*, which was a three-piece white leather sectional. The second was a large twelve-foot straight design with a tweed fabric. These were specially built for teenage ware and tear. The third sofa for the *living room* was standard. A slight curve was wider at one end of the sofa lending style to the design. A beige silk shantung damask material was chosen. It was so beautiful. Quality end tables and coffee tables were purchased to enhance the newly designed sofas. White carpeting, for the living room, large lamps and tables, the bar stools were color matched to the tweed sofa, matching color light fixture over the bar, dinette table for the kitchen with leather upholstery to match the kitchen curtains, short and *small wing back* chairs so that my feet would touch the floor and casters on all chairs. Our formal dinning room with matching chairs came from Fresno. A beautiful birch *game table* was ordered out of Minneapolis and again had casters on the chairs. A beautiful light color fixture was hung above the game table. At last, my long awaited complete set of china and crystal arrived for the dinning room. Topping it all off with beautiful table linens, Sterling Silver Ware, Sterling Platters, Sterling Punch Bowl and Cups and Sterling Candle Stick Holders. It was all so beautiful!

Our master bedroom furniture included a large beautiful *hand crafted* made to order white and gold chest of drawers and two matching night tables with custom brass hardware, a large three winged mirror for the chest, and a king size bed with custom bedding that set off the beauty of our room. Today the set is (44) years old. It has recently been refinished and is positively beautiful. It will never go out of style.

Bedroom furniture and accessories for the boy's rooms was a breeze to find. They were so easy to please.

It was a long process but a delight to watch as everything came together. Eight months later Jack was so proud when the custom sofas with tags reading *Made Especially for Mr. & Mrs. Jack Nutter*, found their place in this beautiful residence. A dream come true for the both of us and what a delight. How Jack loved this house and how we loved him for it.

Getting used to it took some time. When the boys couldn't find me they'd get on the intercom and call out, "Motho, where is yo?" to tease me. And when we invited company to this beautiful abode, we had to remember to notify the gate guards to admit our guests. With a large party we had to acquire gate passes that sported a horse logo. The passes were then returned on to the gate guard as they entered.

We attended church regularly in Rolling Hills, and Jack loved taking us to the Parasol Restaurant for breakfast afterwards. Our Sunday ritual stayed the same, but our vacation trips to Yosemite and Bass Lake were now only memories. It was time to concentrate on our new life in southern California.

Our property included a tennis court, a putting green, an empty horse corral and barn. It took a few months before we found horses suitable for the boys. The first horse we acquired through special advertisement was a Quarter Horse Mare named Dixie. She'd had extensive training in gymkhanas. All we had to do was point her head in the right direction and hang on. *The Texas Barrel* race was magic; Dixie knew exactly what to do, and presto! We had a blue ribbon. She knew about *Tight-Reining*, too; the rider just needed to keep his or her legs tight against Dixie's body and she'd take off between those posts. She made all of us look good, while earning us many blue ribbons. She was smart and beautiful and we were proud to own her. When I had trouble mounting her, she'd lean forward and down in front of me. I'm certain that Dixie thought she was human. She was such a joy to own and ride.

Our next find was Bo, a Black-and-White Mustang Gelding who was a great deal taller than Dixie. Once he was saddled he wanted to go, but he was too energetic and spirited for me. He was a horse strictly for the boys and Dad. They knew how to control him and they traveled along our many horse trails right there in Rolling Hills. Jack loved to watch Bo as he held his head high seemingly with pride. Our many horse shows took place right there in Rolling Hills at Caballeros Del Rancho Palos Verde's, Inc. There were many shows over the years and many blue, white, and yellow ribbons for all of us. Our lives were entirely different,

148

along with a complete change from that of Fresno. It was like starting all over again.

After Thanksgiving, the boys entered their new school. The adjustment wasn't easy for any of them, and for Terry it was especially hard. Not long after he entered Trinity Catholic School, his teacher called me to set up a meeting about our number three son. At our appointment she told me she was contemplating setting Terry backs a grade, and I was shocked. She told me he did nothing in class but sit and stare out the window, never handing in homework, and avoided the other boys. No matter what she said or did he wouldn't respond. She didn't believe for one moment that he was slow or retarded, but felt the class was a detriment to him and that setting him back a grade might be the best course of action. I suspected what the problem was, and asked her to please hold off until I'd had a chance to talk with him. She agreed.

The boys were still sitting at the table after dinner that evening when I casually brought up the subject of school. I asked how they were doing, if they were happy at school, or were having any problems with their homework? All the boys talked about their classes and what they were doing except Terry; all he did was listen. I directed my next question at him. "Since all of you are so happy, which by the way pleases me very much, would any of you boys like to go to Fresno to visit any of your old friends?"

Terry gave me a hard stare and said, "Would you really take us to Fresno to visit our friends, Mom?" "You bet! You can write your friends when we'll be there and invite them to our motel for a swim or whatever you want to do. It would be a treat to take them out to dinner or lunch, whatever they want." Terry's eyes were like saucers and his grin was a mile long. He jumped out of his chair and started off to his room, saying, "I'm going to write my friends **r i g h t** away!"

Out loud I said, "Only under one condition, fellows." Terry returned, saying, "OK, what's the catch?" "No catch," I said, "but since all of you are in new schools, I want to know what your teachers are like. I've been negligent in visiting your classes, and your teachers, and I apologize for that, but it's time for me to do some checking. Dad and I know it hasn't been easy for any of you. After all, you've been pulled out of school in the middle of the year, and I know that can be a big problem. I'd like to visit your classes next week and see what your teachers have to say about your activities. I've been thinking that good reports might deserve a trip to Fresno. How about it? A couple of days in our old hometown would be a treat. I have friends I want to visit, too, you know."

Four of the boys were enthusiastic. "Sure, Mom, come and visit our classes. It hasn't been easy, but it's working out all right." Terry still had his suspicions. "Yeah, and what's Dad going to say about this?" "You just leave Dad to me." He was right Dad was not happy about it, but soon saw the validity of the idea. He consented and the boys jumped for joy, especially Terry.

A week later when I checked on our number three son, his teacher said in total amazement, "Whatever did you say to your son? I can't believe the improvement in his attitude alone; he's an entirely different student." I wasn't surprised, but I was pleased to know that he'd snapped out of his depression. I told her that she didn't have to worry about him any more, that he' would be fine.

Two weeks later Patrick, Terry, Dennis, and I arrived at a motel in Fresno; Jack and Michael had decided to stay home with their father. As soon as we checked in, Terry began calling his friends. One of his best friends wasn't at home but his mother expected him soon. Terry wanted to be there when his friend arrived, so we drove him over to his house. Our plan was that they'd do their thing during the day, and Terry would invite his friend or friends to have dinner with us afterwards. He was to call me, and then I'd pick them up for dinner and possibly a movie. What better plan could we have had?

After most of the day had passed without a word from Terry, I called his friend's house. I spoke with Terry who said we could pick him up any time. We set the time, and then one of Patrick's friends came over to visit him. They had a great time together talking about school and their classmates. We went to lunch and then drove over for Terry and found him waiting for us outside. He didn't look too happy as he got into the car, so I asked if his friend would be joining us for dinner. Sadly, he told us his friend hadn't come home.

"I don't understand Terry, didn't you write him when you were coming?" "Yes, but he had other important things to do." "Well, he's going to be sorry, because it just so happens that we're going to the greatest restaurant and on to a movie afterwards—that is, if it's OK with you. Do you suppose you would like that?" "Yeah! I really would, Mom!"

Terry suffered a rude awakening that day. His friends meant so much to him, yet they seemed to have forgotten about him when he left and they sure did not miss him. He was terribly disappointed, but his brothers and I did our best to make it up to him. Fortunately, Terry was old enough and he had self-confidence in himself to handle his disappointment. His attitude changed completely once we returned to Rolling Hills and back to school. I was ever so proud of him.

Dennis and Michael had entered Dapple-gray Grade School in Palos Verde's. They didn't feel welcome which created problems getting adjusted, but they weren't easily discouraged. We had long talks about their problems; while they helped each other work through them. I marveled over their ability to understand their classmates' attitudes and adjust themselves accordingly. Eventually their peers accepted them; their patience made it all possible and once again I was proud of them.

After Dennis graduated from Dapple-gray Junior High School he entered Miraleste High School and in 1970 was a member of the school's **First** graduating class. That year a group of teenagers vandalized the intersection of Sunset and Vine in Los Angeles. Dennis read about it in the newspaper and said, "I'm so ashamed of my generation, Mom. How could they stoop to this level? Such terrible destruction makes me sick to my stomach. I don't want to be a part of this generation. Don't consider me a teenager, OK, Mom?" I understood his feelings and I too was ashamed for him.

Dennis worked on the local help line, talking to kids who called in for help. His words of wisdom help many troubled teens. I marveled over his ability to do this, and Dad and I supported him in his quest to help others.

Jack Jr. entered Ferman Lasuen High School in 1961. He had grown up to be a fine young man, thoughtful, caring, and considerate to others. He was quick to see the problems of the different teens around him and he discreetly helped those less fortunate than himself. When several of his classmates tried to contaminate him with drugs, he made it very clear that he wasn't interested. Indeed, he did his best to talk to them about its destructiveness.

He did a great job. His wit and humor attracted others to him and he, like his brothers, helped many teens. When Jack graduated from Ferman, his name was engraved on the large gold Honor Roll Plaque at the school's entrance. He was at the top of his class and we marveled over his achievement. Thirty years later, the school board closed Ferman; today the building houses senior citizens.

Jack and I were clear in the message we gave our boys from an early age: NO DRUGS. Over the years we had many conversations with our sons about the devastating results of drug abuse. We pointed out that not only were drugs potentially dangerous, but it would be worse to have to answer to their Dad for using them! Looking back, I believe their father's firm hand had a great influence on them. We always emphasized over and over in our family conferences on the drug issue. We were clear we wouldn't tolerate any of our sons belittling themselves with this problem. In my heart I firmly believed the boys took pride in themselves so much that the idea of drugs Thank God, the boys listened. I was so grateful to Jack for being involved in his sons' lives, and proud of how he handled this crucial matter. I was equally proud of the boys' strength to do the right thing.

Patrick was so interested in golf that nothing else intrigued him. Unfortunately we discovered much later that he was skipping different classes during the week in order to caddy at the Palos Verde's Golf Course on the peninsula. As a result his grade-point average dropped. He did enough schoolwork to get by but it curtailed his ability to enter the college of his choice later. When he went to the club to caddy, many golfers would be waiting for him when he arrived. He was so happy when so many of these important men wanted him to caddy for them. He never wavered from his future career choice of golf, but he was limited.

Dennis wasn't in junior high very long when he decided to build a dune buggy. At thirteen he wasn't old enough to earn a driver's license, but by the time he finished the buggy he would be of age. He enlisted his oldest brother's help and the two of them made plans to build his dream vehicle. All he needed now was an OK from Mom and Dad. When he promised faithfully that the buggy wouldn't interfere with his studies, he got a firm OK!

He started out with a cut-down Volkswagen chassis. When the chassis was delivered we had it stored in the barn so he could work on it in his spare time. He planned to complete the buggy by the time he was sixteen taking his first driving test in his own self-made vehicle. Dad felt that we were spoiling Dennis, but I was eager to see him finish his project. Dennis kept abreast of every available part through *Mechanics Magazine* and we searched for the parts he needed through this magazine. Shopping around for these parts was a joy no matter how far we had to travel to get them.

Not only was Dennis building a car, he was also taking flying lessons at the Torrance Municipal Airport. Locating parts for the dune buggy and driving him back and forth to the airport for his flying lessons were keeping me busy. He wanted to earn both his driver's license along with his pilot's license on his sixteenth birthday. Marvelous ambition for a thirteen-year-old, but the best part is that he accomplished both goals!

The day I drove Dennis, in his Dune Buggy, down Hawthorne Boulevard for his driving test was truly memorable. He was idly waving a toy gun around and telling me how happy he was. "It's happening, Mom! It's really happening!" he said, and playfully pointed the plastic gun at my head. I had no idea he had done that, but I saw a police car with its red lights on in the rear-view mirror and I was puzzled. "Dennis," I said, "what have I done wrong? The police just turned their lights on me and I know I've been obeying traffic rules. Is there a problem with the buggy?" I didn't know what to think. "Just pull over, Mom," he said "the buggy is fine as he casually set the gun underneath his seat. "Let's see what they want."

Two police officers got out of the patrol car and flanked the Dune Buggy. I handed my driver's license to the officer on my left, while the other officer said to Dennis, "You had something in your hand as you were riding along." "Oh yes," said Dennis, and he reached down and picked up the toy gun on the floorboard. In a split second the officer grabbed Dennis's wrist with one hand and snatched the gun with the other. Almost immediately the officer realized the gun was plastic. Both Dennis and I were amazed by the officer's actions. This was the year of 1968. Had this of occurred at his writing 2003 the officers probably would not have been so lenient with my number five son. Dennis apologized immediately.

The officer said, "You pointed this gun at the driver's temple where everybody could see you, and passing cars thought you had a real gun and reported it to the police immediately." "I'm so sorry, sir!" Dennis said as he got out of the car. "I was just playing. This is my Mom and she's taking me for my driver's license, and then we're going to the Torrance Airport for my pilot's license. I guess I was getting too excited!"

The two officers talked with Dennis at length. He told them when he started building the Dune Buggy and why. Along with his school studies he was also taking pilot's lessons over the past three years. The officers were impressed by his attitude, congratulated him heartily on his accomplishments before saying goodbye and good luck. They left and Dennis returned to the passenger seat.

"Mom, this is terrible!" Dennis was so embarrassed. I was, too—Jokingly I said! "Pulled over while driving a Dune Buggy can you imagine!"—But I did my best to soothe his feelings. "Dennis it was a little embarrassing, but funny, too. Those police officers were just as embarrassed as we were, so don't feel bad, honey. Let's go to the DMV, OK?" "Sure Mom." My thoughts, pulled over in a buggy! Enough is enough.

After he passed his written test, our number-five son passed his first driving test in his very own vehicle, the *Dune Buggy*. The instructor just shook his head as Dennis used the bug for his driving test. From there Dennis himself drove the two of us to the airport where Dad was waiting. The photographer from the *Peninsula Breeze* was on hand to take Dennis' picture in the cockpit of the plane before his solo flight. We watched him as he took off in the Cessna 172. Dad told me during the flight that in Dennis' sixteen years he had accomplished a great deal, and this was just the beginning for him. We took a great deal of pride in his accomplishments, and congratulated him. He drove the Bug home with a grin on his face a mile long. He was so happy!

I spent my young years taking care of our sons, letting Dad do his thing. Now the time had come for me to spend my time doing for Dad and being with him. Jack's job had him traveling all over the country, and I went with him every time the opportunity presented itself. Even though the boys were in their teens, I never allowed them to be alone if we were gone for any length of time.

My Mother and Dad always welcomed the thought of staying with them. The boys had plenty of outside activities to keep them busy, and their friends came over constantly. All they were required to do was to keep their grandparents informed as to where they were going and when they were to return. Rules were strictly enforced. We had a twelve o'clock curfew. No if, ands, or buts about it.

**1962
Dennis Paul Nutter
The start of a promising career
with the Constellation Trumpet
he loved.**

**October 23, 1968
Heading for the Department of Motor Vehicles in
Torrance, California for Dennis's Driver Licenses**

Palos Verdes Estates, Rolling Hills, Rolling Hills Estates and all Peninsula Communitie

PENINSULA *Breeze*

Published every Thursday by the South Bay Daily Breeze   10¢ Per Copy, $7.00 Per Year Mailed   Thursday, Oct. 31, 1968

Dennis Nutter, 16, of Rolling Hills, sits at the controls as he prepares to takeoff on his first solo flight at Torrance Municipal Airport. The Miraleste High School football player had to wait for his 16th birthday to solo, and got his flying license ahead of his driver's permit.

It took three years to finish building his Dune Buggy. Regular School, Flight lessons and Trumpet lessons in his spare time. Finally all the requirements were accomplished on his 16th Birthday. The Buggy was completed, Pilot license and Driver license finalized. That day reflected a bright and sunny atmosphere for our number Five Son, Dennis and the entire family.

158

Chapter 21

Rose Bowl Events and Community Affairs

*W*e discovered that Rolling Hills was full of teenagers. I'd always told the boys that we'd give them as much responsibility as they could accept, in the event if the day came when we saw they weren't handling things well, we'd have to intervene. "If your friends don't come up to your standards, the way you were trained, it's your responsibility to walk away, or show them the way. Take your choice. Always feel free to call on us whenever the need arises". They understood and acted accordingly.

Our sons' teenage friends visited our household frequently, and I always made it a point to chat with them. Our game table was in constant use and I listened to every conversation over cards. One particular teen, Mike, was out of order in his behavior, his public activities, and his lack of respect to those around him. The boys themselves did not feel as I did. We knew, of course that Mike's home life was unhappy and I was sympathetic, but there were times when he really made me think twice. One evening while we were having dinner I mentioned that I was aware of his negative attitude and lack of consideration for the boys. I told them, in no uncertain terms, that I wanted them to cut their association with him.

Number-four son Michael grabbed my arm and said, "Mother, take it easy, give us a couple of weeks, we'll have Mike thinking our way." "Two weeks isn't going to do it, fellows. First of all, he thinks you boys are crazy." "Trust us Mom, he really is a good kid," said Patrick. "OK, if that's the way you feel, you got two weeks, but I'll be keeping a watchful eye."

A month passed, and I asked the boys after dinner one evening, "Fellows, what's going on? Your two weeks are up." Jack spoke up immediately. "We didn't think you'd ever ask us, Mom. Believe it when we say that this is a great kid. You're going to love him." "I don't believe it, I said, but I hope you're right. Time will tell."

Prior to this conversation I'd conferred with Dad about the problem with this boy. I was worried that our sons wouldn't be able to handle this sort of situation, and I asked him to do something. He told me not to worry, that he'd take care of it.

A few days later the neighborhood teens were invited to our house to play football. Dad joined in the game, and when it ended I served snacks and soft drinks. Just before they finished eating, Dad asked if he could talk with all of them on a personal basis. "Sure, why not?" was their reply. He talked about their future aspirations, saying that the cost of their education would never be a problem; their parents would see to that so, they should all reach for the sky. He touched on the use of foul language, disrespect, and lack of consideration for their peers. He talked about the drug scene. "In later years when you look back on your lives, how will you feel about your accomplishments?" He posed this question and looked around at the boys. They stared back and slowly nodded their heads. This was the beginning of many football "sessions" and all the kids looked forward to them. Dad was so in tune with those boys; they really loved him and respected him.

Sure enough, Mike turned out great. He finally realized where he was heading if he didn't change. He learned to control his temper and to respond respectfully to adults and his peers. He thought before he acted and was on his best behavior wherever he went. I know it had to be difficult for him, but he was determined. We all learned to love him. He was only one of many that were helped by our boys—and, of course, Dad's input was worth its weight in gold.

In Dad's line of work, he was often given tickets to ball games, movie theaters, and you name it. On New Year's Day 1962 he took the whole family to the Rose Bowl in Pasadena. I bought the boys special red shirts and blue trousers; what better colors for such a large crowd? We were lucky to get seats on the 50-yard line. Perfect location, but the seats weren't together. There were

160

three seats above and four seats below, with five rows between them. Well, the boys had it all planned: the older boys rated the lower seats and Mom, Dad and Dennis rated the upper seats. Fair enough, I guess; at least that way I could keep an eye on them.

As I looked over that huge crowd, I realized that not only did our boys have on red shirts but a trillion other men; women and children wore the same color. What a dilemma! Several young girls saw the boys dressed alike and assumed they were famous. "Now who ... let's see ... of course, you're famous for TV commercials, right?" The boys just grinned. "What movies were you in?" The grins broadened. Other curious folks accosted them, and the boys gobbled up all the attention and played the game to the hilt. Needless to say, they had a ball the entire day.

Michael was enthralled with this and as he scanned the crowd, he cooked up some ideas of his own. President Dwight Eisenhower was the honorary Grand Marshall of the Rose Bowl that year, and our number-four son wanted his autograph. The President sat just below the boys on the 50-yard line. Michael managed to get past the security agents, but one of them spotted him as he approached the President. The agent reached out to grab him, but the President shook his finger and his head, saying, "No, it's OK." With that, Michael said, "Mr. President, may I have your autograph?" and handed him his seating ticket. President Eisenhower graciously obliged with a borrowed pen and handed the ticket back to Michael, who snapped to attention, saluted smartly, and said, "Thank you, Mr. President!" before an agent ushered him quickly away.

You'd think that was enough for our boy, but no. He spotted Dick Van Dyke and his wife sitting close by, so Michael bambustled over to them and asked the actor to autograph his ticket. As Mr. Van Dyke readied his pen, he said, "Wow, I'm honored. I get to sign right next to our President." Michael grinned from ear to ear as Mr. Van Dyke signed and returned his ticket, "Thank you, sir!" says Mike as he bowed deeply. What a ham he was and everyone loved him!

In the meantime I could hardly see where the boys were. So many red shirts! I wore myself out trying to find them. Dad told me to relax, that the boys wouldn't let us get very far from them, and besides the game was about to start. If you can't beat 'em, join 'em, so I settled down to enjoy the game.

I was hooked on football long before then, but that day was very special. When the game ended we all got back together, and the boys thanked Dad for getting the tickets for them. They told him what a great time they'd had and asked if we could do it again next year. Dad smiled, saying it was a long way off but surely he'd have to give it some serious consideration. Did we do it again the following year? You bet!

In 1963 I was asked to be chairman of the annual Rolling Hills Christmas ball, in which all the residents participated in one way or another. I accepted and promptly set up a committee to assist me. We scheduled the affair at the Palos Verde's Country Club, and the chef agreed to prepare baked Alaska for dessert. I ordered centerpieces for the dining tables: white lace butterflies on three- and four-foot wire stems, which were scheduled to set in red aza-leas plants donated by the local florist. I also ordered six white turbans and six white aprons, all of which were made by commit-tee members, and I rented a set of black-light fixtures from a local electric company.

When the time came to install the black lights, there wasn't a man available to help. I was frantic; time was of the essence. Already the girls had seventy-five butterflies made, six turbans, six special aprons, and the florist was ready to deliver the red aza-leas. I underwent what one might call a crisis of confidence. After dinner that night I appealed to Dad for help. I explained every-thing, adding that I was at my wit's end. He patiently listened to me and said, "Well, fellows, what are we going to do about this? Mother needs help." A few more questions were asked and then I heard the magic words: "We'll do it for you, Mom!" I protested, it is a difficult installation, and there is very little time. Our sons confidently assured me they could handle it, and if not, they'd find someone who could.

Dad rented tremendous ladders to reach the high ceiling in the clubhouse banquet room. I watched nervously, worried about everything, but Dad had the situation under control. Our boys went to work while the committee set up twenty-five tables and placed the centerpieces. The men wearing the turbans and the women wearing the special aprons rehearsed their routines. When the boys finished the installation, we tested the lights. Everything was absolutely beautiful—the turbans, aprons, lace butterflies, red azaleas, all of it. Impressed with the overall effect, we happily but wearily called it a day.

The festivities started Saturday night with no-host cocktail parties in individual homes. Afterwards we all headed for the clubhouse, where the entire committee took their places to greet our guests. The band played soft music as we all drifted to the dining tables. After everyone was seated, I picked up the microphone, thanked everyone for joining us, and then thanked my committee members one by one. I then introduced the club's president as the staff began serving dinner.

Once dinner was over and the crowd started to settle down, fanfare introduced the arrival of dessert. When the main lights were extinguished the black lights came on. I found myself holding my breath. The staff marched in and continued around the tables, carrying the Flaming Baked Alaska high over their heads as the band played in the background. It was a spectacular sight, and the crowd loved it. Applause thundered through the clubhouse and echoed back again.

I wore a blue beaded gown with white teardrop pearls. The dangling gems shimmered and glistened under the black light as Dad and I kicked off the dancing. As he took me into his arms, I whispered my thanks in his ear. Dad smiled and said, "It's my pleasure, Mrs. Nutter, and I thank you, too." I could see that he was practically bursting with pride. It was a most beautiful evening.

As the evening drew to a close, we announced that a bright red dot had been placed under one saucer on each table. Each centerpiece belonged to the person whose saucer had the red dot. After the tables were cleared and the centerpieces claimed, we bid good night to everyone as they were leaving the ballroom.

I felt so good—so relieved!—that the affair was such a great success. Everyone had worked very hard through months of planning. Our boys were there when I needed them again. So many times over the years Dad had spoken sternly to me, about various things but never did he ever yell or raise his voice. This particular evening he was thoughtful, considerate, and loving. I was ever so grateful for his patience, his help, and his endearing words.

Just before leaving the Rose Bowl Game in Pasadena, Calif.
Pat and Terry 1962 with Mom on Crutches

Jacks first Lincoln Continental 1963

Half Time Trojans on the Field

Chapter 22

One Storm, Two Convertibles

*I*n 1962, Jack seemed to be forever traveling around the country. I was always driving to LAX, the Los Angeles International Airport, to drop him off or pick him up. Being gone so much of the time, he made it a point to call home frequently. Often, to his frustration, he couldn't reach us because the telephone was busy almost constantly. After returning home, one evening Dad angrily expressed how he felt and announced that he wanted a private unlisted number, one the boys would be forbidden to use. "I hope you boys understand my frustration," he said. We all nodded. "Mother, call the telephone company tomorrow and ask them to install a new line." Then to our sons he said, "With the new phone, you may only answer it. After all, it'll be me calling."

Jack made frequent trips to Hawaii. He was setting up a new subsidiary, which required constant attention. Work was so intense at the office that he often worked in his hotel room for hours. During this time he was staying at the beautiful Kahala Hilton. One afternoon the hotel announced a tropical storm warning on their loud speaker. When the storm suddenly developed into a hurricane, the hotel patrons were bussed to a safer place to wait out the danger. Jack, single-minded as he was, was so engrossed in his paperwork that he never even noticed the evacuation. He was aware of the rain and wind outside, but that was nothing to him, so he continued to work.

Hunger pangs finally set in, as he ventured down to the restaurant. When he exited the elevator the hotel was like a tomb; there was no one in sight in that beautiful lobby. He went to the registration desk and hit the service bell, calling out as he looked behind the desk. Complete silence. He said to himself, "OK, let's try the restaurant." As he walked across the floor with his comfortable shoes they seem to click briskly on the shiny tile floor loud and clear, he thought to himself, I've never heard my shoes do that before; what in heaven's name is going on here? The restaurant, main entrance, and bellhop station were all empty. Only then did he realize that something was terribly wrong, but what? Bewildered, he froze in his tracks, wondering, am I suppose to get some kind of message here? He decided to return to his room to make some calls and get some answers.

As he headed for the elevator a Hilton bus pulled up at the front entrance. People poured out and hurried into the hotel. Dad called out to a lady racing to the elevator: "Please, may I ask, what's going on here?" "It's OK now she said, the hurricane has by-passed us, and now it's safe to return to your room." He thanked her as a cold chill flowed up and down his spine; shocked to realize the danger he'd been in. Then his face lit up like a Christmas tree with the knowledge that he'd been spared. He suddenly remembered ignoring the loudspeaker announcement instructing all patrons to go to the lobby. Transportation to safety was of the essence but because he was so engrossed in his paper work he ignored the announcement..

He called home later that day and said, "Honey, a funny thing happened to me on the way to the restaurant today." He then told me the whole story. We both laughed about it, but it wasn't funny, and I thanked God that he was safe.

For Christmas in 1962 Felixie's made there way under the Christmas tree. A Felixie is like a snow sled. They have hand brakes in front and a bar across the front, which guides the four wheels down the road as the child glides on his stomach usually on the right side of the pavement. Jackie was racing down Chesterfield when his Felixie hit a rock. The Felixie flipped in the air and Jackie landed on his collar bone (clavicle) and had to wear a brace for weeks. The pain was excruciating, but he never complained. Pat was coming down Chesterfield on his stomach unable to slow down and went flying under the neighbors' fence. The Felixie was out of control as he flew in the air and down the steep canyon. Fortunately Jackie witnessed the incident and helped Pat out of the canyon. The boys did not tell me what happened, but the neighbors did. Before any one got seriously hurt I tied the

Felixies together, hung them in the corner of the garage and dared the boys to use them again. Today Felixies are outlawed.

Later in our busy lives, on a Saturday afternoon in 1963, Dad announced to me that he wanted to buy a new car. I said jokingly, "Be patient and Dennis will have one for you very soon."

"I'm serious, Mom."

"OK, what kind of car?" I asked.

"I believe I'd like to own a new Lincoln Continental Convertible."

"A what?" I said, then jokingly added, "Dennis's dune buggy will be a convertible.

"Come on, Mom. Do you have any objections to a Lincoln?"

"No, you already complain about my hair, in a convertible I'll look like a porcupine."

"In that case, let's look for a car for you, too!"

"No, no, thank you honey, my car is fine right now."

"Well, I'd like to look around. Want to go with me? If not, I'll take Jack. What do you think?" "I have lots to do here at home, so the two of you can take time to look around. You *do just want to look around right?"* "Right! "OK then." So he called for Jack, and in minutes both of them were gone. For a moment there I thought it was strange that he casually asked me to go with him; usually he doesn't ask me, he tells me. But then I thought I was probably making something out of nothing, so I put it out of my mind.

Almost five hours had passed when I saw a beautiful white Lincoln Continental Convertible entering our driveway with Dad behind the wheel, a grin on his face a mile long. I couldn't believe my eyes. Right behind him was a bright red Chevrolet Impala Convertible driven by number-one son Jack. The boys and I ran out of the house for a closer look. Then Dad's famous words: "How do you like it, honey?"

I really was in a state of shock. "Like it? What do you mean? Really, honey, you're kidding, right? You didn't buy two cars, and convertibles to boot? What kind of thinking possessed you to do this?

The consequences of a teenager driving a car is bad enough, but a convertible! Couldn't you call me? At lease give me a chance to express myself? If I did this without your permission you'd be furious with me! "He said, Really honey, I thought you'd be

169

pleased. After all, now you don't have to do all the driving. Jack is going to be happy to help you, right, son?"

"You got it right this time, Dad."

"Besides, I couldn't just go out and buy one car for myself and not one for our son too!"

"Really?" I walked around both cars, eyeing them. "Remember our first car, honey? It was a beat-up '35 Ford with so many dents and scratches it reminded me of the U.S. map. A cog on the starter was broken, the roof leaked, the windshield would blow open at the slightest wind and would blew water in my face or dirty dust." They all looked at me as if they thought I was crazy, so I asked what had happened to Jack's car. When he told me he'd traded it in for the Lincoln, I groaned. "Why do I get the feeling I'm dreaming?" Jackie said, "It's for real, Mom. They belong to us. Dad had to sign all the paperwork before we left the dealer. And Mom, you should've been there with us, it was so much fun!" "Yes Jack, I wish I would have been there." (Today *the law states that every vehicle on the road and everyone in the vehicle is subjected to wearing seat belts.*) Back then; there were no seat belts.

"OK," I said wearily, "how much did you pay, and how much is it going to cost us on monthly payments?" My head spun with the thought of the expense. Dad said, "Relax, Mom, we paid cash. Right, Jack!" "Right, Dad!" "Cash?" I shouted. "Jackie, how could you let your father do this?" "Mom, I tried to stop him, but he kept insisting it was what he wanted to do."

I was fit to be tied. With what little driving Jack had done, I could see he was pretty cautious and very obedient to traffic rules, but nevertheless I really wanted him to wait a little longer before we put him behind the wheel of his own automobile. I had my hands over my mouth as I croaked, "A convertible, and two of them. What next?" Then Dad said, "Mom, look here, you just touch a button and the top goes up or down. Want to see how easy it is? You're going to love driving this car. With me gone so much, the car is yours." "Thanks a lot," I said sourly.

"You'd better call our insurance agent tomorrow, Mother, and cover these cars." He pointed to the Impala. "Jack, that car will sit until it's covered by sufficient insurance, OK?" "OK, Dad."

I couldn't believe this was happening, but there was no point in arguing about it. Buying auto insurance for a teenager was not a breeze. I had to listen to our agent about teenage driving and all the problems sixteen-year-olds cause on the road.

Prior to the new cars the boys had unicycles. They'd take them to school and ride them to their classes. But once the Impala made its appearance, the unicycles were never used again. After that Jack was always driving his brothers to one place or another in his new red sharpshooter. That was a lot of responsibility and he loved it. Every morning without fail he'd dust the car off before it left the garage. I'd wave goodbye—and say a silent prayer for their safety.

At one point Jackie transmission was erratic. We talked about it but we could not define the problem. So, I decided it was best to have the car towed to the Chevrolet dealer where the car was purchased. I spoke to the Manager at length and I convinced him that they sold us a lemon. Because of this it was their duty to replace the transmission at no cost to us. They apologized and agreed. When we picked up the car, the mechanic who had replaced the transmission said he was puzzled. He found strange motor shavings in the bottom of the transmission case. He could not understand how that could possibly happen and I didn't have a clue.

Well guess what? It was not long when it happened again and I was fit to be tied. "What is going on Jack? Chevrolet will not replace another transmission." Terry said, "Jack you had better tell Mom." "Tell me what?" "Well", Jack said, "it's like this." The story came out that he was taking the car to the drag races and racing an automatic vehicle, converting the speed to a standard gear. Consequently the transmission could not take it without severe damage. "Unbelievable," I said. "OK Jack, I wash my hands. It is now your responsibility. If you want this car back to normal, it will be paid completely by you. Don't get any ideas for funds from me or from Dad. He is not going to be happy when you have to face him with the truth!" Jackie knew exactly what he had to do. He worked extra hours in order to replace the transmission. After that Jackie and the Impala got along just fine. The only time I was allowed to drive his car was when he was low on gas. On my return one day he casually ventured to the car to check his gas gage. He wasn't fooling me!

The boys seem to have inherited Dad's ability to be calm in their actions. They think before they speak. Never as adults have I ever heard any of them yell or scream at anyone. They love and respect their families and friends. They never use bad language, and they don't consume alcohol in abundance. As teenagers they did experiment with cigarettes, but not for long; it was a passing fancy for them and too expensive. They've never used illegal drugs, and that alone makes me fall to my knees with gratitude. They're not perfect, but they constantly set good examples and they work well with people. What more could I expect? Jack was so proud of his sons, and frequently told them so.

For a while, Jackie worked for Taco Bell on weekends. One afternoon on his way home he was pulled over by the San Pedro police, who asked him for his license, registration, and proof of auto insurance. (*At that time, auto insurance was not compulsory*) "Officer," said Jack, "May I ask why I've been stopped?" The officer looked into the car and saw a little white toy dove on a long spring that "flew" just below Jack's dashboard. The officer lifted it with his hand and it flew softly in the air. Jack said, "My Dad said that as long as that dove doesn't fly above the dashboard, it's OK." The officer replied, "Your Dad's right, but if I look long enough I'll find something here that will warrant a ticket." He then checked the tires, brakes, radiator, front and rear bumpers, lights, directional signals and even the windshield wipers. He could find nothing wrong, and grudgingly let Jack go. As Jack drove off he called out to the officer and said, "Thank you, officer!" When he got home he told us about his experience. I was furious! "Did you get his badge number?" I demanded. "No, I didn't, Mom, but if he stops me again I just might do that!"

Early one morning Jack and Patrick were driving down Miraleste, a divided road, heading for school. Toward the end of the road and at the first intersection a camper heading the opposite direction made an immediate left turn into Jack's lane without looking or stopping. Jack applied his brakes to avoid smashing into the camper and the Impala went out of control. Crossing the east side of the road through a fence and literally smashing into a gigantic tree which stopped the car. Jack and Pat got out of the car in a state of shock. The camper kept going and was never sited. I was called and when I arrived at the accident scene the two boys were talking with the police. I made arrangements for the car to be towed for repairs and the boys and I returned home. Dad was in Los Angeles heading a conference with delegates from all over the country as he was handed a note about the accident. He hurried the session along, excused himself and rushed home. Jackie took the accident very hard and it took sometime for him to regain his composure and confidence. We were grateful the boys were not injured. It took three weeks before the Impala was returned. It looked like new and it ran like a dream. Thank God the car was insured.

Dad and the boys spent a great deal of time discussing school, their homework, their cars, and their futures, particularly what studies would benefit them most in their chosen fields. Most importantly, they loved to play together; football, basketball, golf, cards, and chess. When Dad received compliments about one of the boys, he'd tell me about it with such pride. I recall numerous such days with fond memories.

Our love for each other made us what we are today. I am profoundly grateful to have lived such a full and wonderful life with my husband and our sons. I made a home for my five boys and I did everything possible to keep them and my husband happy. At times it was a real challenge. It was hard work, but with God's help and a bit of good luck along the way I believe I accomplished my goal.

The Hawaiian Village Presentation of a Beautiful Pearl and Black Onyx Pin Presented to Rachel from Emma Lines.

Presentation Award of a *Tiki Salad Bowl* from My Dearest Friend Emma Lines.

Chapter 23

Vacation in Honolulu

$\mathcal{B}$y 1962, Jack's travels were getting to me. I felt it was unhealthy for him to be away so much, especially now that our boys were in their teens. Our conferences about this did not seem to be getting anywhere. He knew I was upset and promised he'd try to do something. "Like what?" I prodded. "I'm not sure," he said, "let me think about it." The next few days were extremely busy at the office and he came home late every night, but at least he would call beforehand so we wouldn't wait dinner for him. My frustration grew as my temper shortened about his being gone so much and he knew it. He really felt bad about this.

In the middle of the night I felt him shaking the bed to wake me. "Honey, look what I have for you." I tried to open my eyes as he pulled a beautiful iridescent nightgown from a box. He held it up and said "How do you like this? You don't?" He threw it on the floor and said, "How about this one then? No? Well, how about this one?" as he pulled out another and then another. Finally I was able to focus my eyes and asked, "Where did you get those gowns?" "I went shopping for you today. The saleslady showed me at least a dozen gowns. I picked out four that I was sure you'd like, and bought them." As he was getting ready for bed he added, "If you don't like them, you're permitted to exchange them to your liking." It was so late, and I was so tired and still angry with him, that I forgot to say thanks. Nevertheless, he still hugged me and told me he loved me.

Early in his career and back in Fresno he did the same thing. This time as he was shaking the bed as he was yelling, *just open your eyes.* "Come on honey, open your eyes." Gradually I saw a flood of five and ten dollar bills falling down around me. I closed my eyes again and said "I know you did not rob a bank, but please tell me about it in the morning. I'm so tied." "It's all yours honey. You can buy a hat or shoes or what ever you want." In the morning he explained that he picked a number on a <u>Lotto Football Game</u> at a cost of five dollars. He had picked the number 23. Weeks later after the game was over he reappeared at the club and the bartender called out to him. ***"Nutter, where have you been? I have something for you."*** As he handed Jack an envelope full of bills the bartender told him he won the "Football Pot". He was alone on number 23 which meant that he won the whole pot. Jack was so shocked with disbelief; he tipped the bartender and rushed home. As I was counting the bills in the morning I said, "Wow honey, this is a lot of money." "Yes and it's yours." "Mine, gee thanks honey." "Tell me, why did you pick the number 23?" "Oh, my birth year seemed perfect, and the only number standing alone on the chart" "You're right honey, it was a perfect number." I was so elated I spent the money on five identical button down shirts for the boys' and a matching one for Dad. Dad felt that I should have spent the money on something that I wanted, but he and the boys loved their new shirts and I loved seeing the six of them all dressed alike. That is what I wanted.

My being angry with him was something he found difficult to tolerate, so he did everything he could to ease the tension. I felt that if I stayed angry with him for a while, or made him think I was angry, he'd come to his senses. I knew for a fact he could get help at his office, but it was up to him to make that decision. So I used my anger to get him to think in a positive way. At one point I told him that there were things that needed to be done around the house and he needed to accept some of the responsibility to get them done. His contention was if he spent time working on incidentals at home it would cheat him from his work at the office, therefore, I was to call those who were better qualified. He wouldn't even change a light bulb. Trying to get him to work around the house, or being angry with him just was not working, but I continued to try. He did like to tinker on the workbench in the washroom area from time to time. That he really enjoyed.

Again he had to leave, and we hardly spoke as I drove him to the airport. I loved him so much that part of me didn't want to be angry with him, but in all honesty, I couldn't help being upset. He felt the tension, but still reached over to hug and kiss me goodbye. "I love you honey, I really do," he said. "Please try to remember I'm doing this for you and the boys." "It's not true; you are doing it for yourself!" "Be patient with me honey, I will call you!"

Before leaving on long trips, he invariably recorded his favorite music for us to listen to while he was gone. He would sing western songs to the boys. Anything that would pop into his head he sang to me. I loved his music, I loved him; I simply was selfish enough to want him home more.

After he'd returned from San Francisco this time he was unpacking his suitcase in our bedroom and he said he had something for me. He pulled a small box from his case and said, "This is for you honey." As I reached for it, I felt he was trying to buy my good will with a gift. I opened the box and saw a beautiful cluster-of-pearls and diamond ring. Jack was just about to close our door when Michael appeared, and at that same moment I threw the ring at Dad, crying, "I don't want your gifts! Remember what you said? You promised you would curtail your traveling!" Michael was stunned. "Mother, how could you?" Jack said, "It's OK, Mike, don't worry," as he closed the door.

That was the first time in all the years of our marriage that any of our boys ever saw me angry with their father. I really felt bad about it, because I'd worked so hard to keep our problems within the confines of our own room. "See what you made me do!" I cried. "Aren't you ashamed of yourself?"

"Me?" pointing to himself, he said as he reached down to pick up the ring. Then he gave me that silly grin, hugged me, and said, "Oh come on, honey, you can't be upset. Please be patient with me. Once I get these subsidiaries on their feet, I won't be traveling so much. Does that make you feel better? But remember, the responsibility right now is mine. It won't be long, and then you'll get tired of me." "Never!" I shot back. As he set the ring back in the box, he said, "Don't worry, I'll return it tomorrow."

One Friday evening in June, Jack came home from work not in one of his best moods. We were watching TV after dinner when he looked over at me and said, "I have to return to Hawaii for another two weeks." He paused for a minute and said, "How would you and the boys like to go with me this time? I'm so tired of being away so much of the time. It'd be great to have the six of you there with me.

I can work in the day and be with you and boys in the evening. What do you think?"

"The boys will be thrilled to death, and you know me honey, traveling with you is the best medicine for me."

"OK. Why don't you plan on reservations for the seven of us? You can make two first-class reservations and five economy reservations for the boys. Give me a couple of days and I'll have the dates for you."

"Economy?"

"Yes. The stewardesses can take over the boys. They'd love all the attention."

"OK, I'll tell them tomorrow, and see what reaction I get."

Summer vacation was just around the corner anyway, so this was a great time to announce Dad's plans. The next evening, just before he came home, I told the boys Dad had to return to Hawaii for a couple of weeks. I spoke to boys in turn, as they all sat around the dinner table, asking them if they'd like to go to Hawaii with us. I believe they thought I was kidding. At that moment Dad came bouncing in the front door, and Jack greeted his father with, "Is there any truth to this Hawaii trip, Dad?" With a big grin on his face and that twinkle in his eye he said, "Would you guys like to go?" All five of the boys exploded into happy chatter, flooding Dad with questions in their excitement. I told them to calm down, that we'd make our plans after we got our reservations.

United Airlines served us well. The boys were seated close together in the plane and not too far behind first class. I checked on them from time to time until Dad said, "Mom, leave those boys alone! They're having a ball." "I simply wanted to see how they were taking the flight," I sniffed.

Our arrival in Hawaii was one of the happiest moments in the boys' lives. After all the traveling we've done together over the years, this was like the top of the Christmas tree. We were laden with leis, one on top of the other. Dad's office personnel greeted us at the airport and he introduced each one of the boys: Jack, number-one son; Patrick, number-two son; and so on. The boys were so courteous it was a pleasure having them with us.

We checked in The Waikiki Beach Tower. Their apartments had breath-taking views of the Pacific and we rented two apartments with balconies and kitchen privileges overlooking the beach. The second apartment was slightly smaller. Dennis and Michael shared the larger apartment with Dad and yours truly; while Jack Jr., Patrick and Terry occupied the apartment next to ours. The boys were so excited to have their own apartment—especially when they discovered a basket full of island fruit on the dining table! The hotel was located at the east end of Waikiki along the beach where the boys could walk to the beach, the shops, or their favorite Burger King where they hung out with newfound friends.

After we'd unpacked, I took the boys shopping at the Ala Moana Shopping Mall where we spent our time and money at Sears. The weather was so hot and humid and running around in Hawaiian attire was something the boys were looking forward to. We purchased matching Hawaiian shirts, shorts, five straw hats, and gifts for the boys' friends back home.

The boys got carried away one afternoon as they looked out toward Waikiki Beach from their fourth-floor balcony. They'd bought balloons on their shopping tour, and the temptation was simply too great. In an instant they were dropping water bombs over the balcony and watching them explode on the busy sidewalk below. One misguided missile landed on a gentleman's head as he was leaving the hotel, drenching him. He looked up just in time to see the boys' heads vanish from the balcony. In seconds this man was pounding on the boys' door. I heard the commotion and opened my door exactly when the boys opened theirs, not realizing what they'd done. The words that flowed out of this man's mouth were not what the boys wanted me to hear. Patrick had a towel ready to use if it was needed. The man grabbed it and yelled at me about what had happened and why was I allowing them to do such a terrible thing. I apologized profusely and so did the boys, with a promise that they'd never do it again. The man stomped off; fortunately he didn't report the incident to the hotel.

I was so embarrassed and angry! I slammed their apartment door behind me and let them have it with both barrels. "What in the world were you thinking? Not one of you boys can leave this room the rest of the day! No television, either; no beach, no nothing!" They tried to apologize, but I refused to be placated. "When Dad comes home you're going to have to answer to him." They made no effort to leave their apartment. I believe they were so embarrassed they were glad to stay in this secure little hideaway.

In the meantime Dennis and Michael were down on the beach where Michael was trying to get one of the men to play chess with him. The beach had Quonset huts where the seniors and tourists could sit at the tables and benches to play chess or cards. When they saw eleven-year-old Michael trying to find a chess partner, they simply ignored him. Michael came home in the evening very disappointed that no one would take him on. But then late one afternoon, as he was ready to return to the apartment again, an elderly gentleman called over to him and asked, "Can you really play chess, kid?" "Yes, sir" was his reply, "and my name is Michael." "OK" said the man, "let's set up the chess board and let's see what you can do." Michael told Dennis to be on the look-out for Mother's flashing light. When I was ready to serve lunch or dinner I'd flash the balcony light off and on, and seeing these lights they were to return to our apartment immediately. Chess takes time, so Dennis placed himself where he could see our balcony. When the lights flashed Dennis told Michael dinner was ready. "I'll go up to the apartment and tell Mother you're playing chess and you'll come home just as soon as the game is over." "Thanks, Dennis."

That little incident created a great deal of interest amongst the people there, and before long quite an audience was watching Michael maneuver his chessmen! Michael lost the first set and asked for a chance to get even. His opponent was so impressed with our number-four son that he agreed.

There was so much to do in the apartment that I simply forgot about Michael's whereabouts. When Dad arrived I naturally filled him in on the day's activities. He realized my patience was in short supply. He went to the boy's apartment and got the story straight. They told him they were just having fun and hadn't meant to hit anyone with the loaded balloon. Dad just took his "Jack Benny" stance: he folded his left arm inward, rested his right elbow in his left hand, held his chin with his right hand, and stood there shaking his head. He felt they'd already served their penance, punishment enough for this vacation. He smoothed everything out with the boys but assured them he wouldn't take it so lightly next time. As he was leaving he turned and said, "I trust you boys haven't forgotten where you are?" The boys answered, "No, and thanks, Dad."

We then realized that Michael wasn't home yet and his dinner was still on the stove. Just about that time the door flew open and our star player was jumping with glee. He described the wonders of the afternoon exuberantly between mouthfuls. He'd beaten his opponent in the second game; then an onlooker had challenged him and lost. Michael then excused himself by telling the crowd that his family was waiting dinner for him. He tried to accept his victory like a gentleman, but actually he was bursting inside. He knew he'd have any number of players to challenge from that day on.

Our Friends Mr. and Mrs. John Lines had arranged a fishing trip for the boys. In my excitement I chose to take movies with our 16 mm movie camera while the boat was fighting the harsh waves. Up and down went the camera and very soon I lost my senses. As I was leaning over the boat coughing up my cookies Dennis said to Dad, "Please Dad, can't you help Mom." Dad said, "Mom is doing what she has to do." I wanted to die. I went below to lie down and the world started to spin. Jackie came below and told me that Mr. Lines was returning to the harbor. "Oh Jack, just let me die in piece," I said: Arriving at the harbor, Jack, Jackie and I. headed for the hotel and off to bed for the rest of the day. Mr. Lines, Pat, Terry, Mike and Dennis fished the rest of the day. They caught nothing but it was fun and they had a great time. Seasickness is so horrendous.

One evening we were all invited to dine at a very famous Japanese restaurant. Various large tropical fish, waterfalls, and the like surrounded us. We had to remove our shoes and wear kimonos. When the boys were younger they'd been introduced to Japanese food, but this meal was elegantly served in different stages. We sat on floor cushions as the waitresses, all in Japanese attire, served us in kneeling positions. When the men were served Sake, (Japanese Liquor) the boys acted very grown up and suggested they wouldn't mind trying it themselves. "It would be a new experience and a welcome treat," they said with a smile. The waitress smiled, too, and brought them Coca-Cola in bottles. The boys kept the bottles, which they later used as telescopes. The boys joked about their attire and had fun all evening while Dad continued with business as usual and I visited with my dear friend Emma Lines during the evening. As we departed the restaurant the boys graciously thanked Dad's associates for inviting them. The boys then graciously invited them to visit us in California as we bid everyone goodnight.

On another evening Dad took us to dinner at the Hawaiian Village to see the Don Ho show. It reminded the boys of the times we'd taken them to different floorshows in Fresno. After the show Dad drove us back to our hotel, singing snatches of Hawaii music and "Tiny Bubbles."

It was a wonderful two weeks, and none of us wanted it to end. Nevertheless, everybody did their own packing and before we knew it we were off to the airport, where Dad's office personnel again covered us with beautiful leis. The boys made the rounds, thanking everyone for their hospitality. Compliments about our sons' behavior made both Dad and I very proud of them. One of the associates, Mr. Charlie Fugitani, approached me and said that he'd like to ask me a very personal question. I nodded OK. "It's been such a pleasure meeting these boys and what I'd like to know is, how were you able to train all these young men to be so polite, and such gentlemen?" Before I could answer, Jack Jr. snapped to attention and said, "I can answer that question, sir!" Mr. Fugitani burst out laughing, but quickly composed himself and said, "OK, Mr. Nutter, let's hear it."

"My mother was a very strict disciplinarian. When she said no, we could never get a yes out of her no matter how hard we tried. We couldn't go to Dad for help, either. We were doomed whether we liked it or not, so we resigned ourselves. But she always worked extra hard at making it up to us, and buttered us up with a lot of TLC. We always went to bed happy and with a full stomach no matter how hard or how strict the day turned out!"

Mr. Fugitani smiled broadly. "Well, I guess it would've had to be like that. That's great, Jack. Thanks." He shook Jack's hand, then mine, and we heard our flight being announced. We said our final alohas and boarded the plane, with all the boys wearing their Hawaiian attire.

The following Christmas, nearly a year later, as everybody was opening their holiday gifts Dennis pulled a box from way under the tree. "Mom, here is something for you." The tag reads "To Mom with Love from Dad." I opened it to find another package, beautifully wrapped. There were four packages in all and as everybody watched me open each package the excitement mounted. The first three were words of love, but when I opened the last package I found a beautiful diamond ring, which had a cluster-of-pearls surrounding the diamond. The boys said, "Wow, Mom, you're sure lucky!" I told Dad, as I slipped it on my finger, "It's beautiful, honey and it's the right size. Thank you."

Dad had a huge amazing grin on his face, and his body was shaking. "What's so funny?" the boys asked as they turned to look at me. "Gee," I said, "I don't know." Dad was laughing really hard at this point. "Come on, tell us, what's so funny, Dad?" He refused to answer until I'd promised not to be angry with him. "I'm not angry with you, honey" nevertheless I hesitated, confused, until the boys clamored, "We want to laugh too, so come on, Mom, promise!" I did, with a silly grin on my face, and Jack, still laughing, said, "Well, remember the time when I returned from San Francisco, and I brought you a gift?"

"You did?"

"Yes. You threw it at me in the bedroom." Michael jumped in: "I remember that."

"Well, what you have on your finger is what you threw at me." I hardly knew what to say, but I couldn't help but laugh with him. "You told me that you were going to return it to the store!"

"Right, but I didn't." "Where on earth have you kept it all this time?"

"I kept it in my desk at the office, Top drawer, Left corner." Michael said, "That'll teach you, Mom." I replied, *"That just shows to go you, fellows, it never pays to try and get the upper hand with Dad—__he always wins!__"* It was such a beautiful ring and I wore it constantly.

All of Jack's necessary personal items were taken care of as holidays, birthdays and the like rolled around, but not once did it occur to me to present something really special to my husband. Suddenly I felt negligent and it was time to take action. One evening after work while we were sitting on the couch in the family room, I presented him with a fancy wrapped package. He said, "What is this? It's not my birthday. It's not our anniversary." Just open it. I told him. As he did he found to his delight a beautiful one-carat diamond stickpin with quarter-carat matching diamond cufflinks! "You like them?" I asked. As he was placing the stickpin in his tie, he said, "I love them, honey! They must have

185

been expensive?" Jokingly I said, "If they don't appeal to you can exchange them." We both laughed. "I had them made especially for you honey!" "I'm not surprised, and thank you Mrs. Nutter. You didn't have to do this, but I'm glad you did." I couldn't help but feel a burst of pleasure at that moment. He loved them and he wore them every day.

Over the years, I worked hard to keep calm and collected when dealing with the boys. Whenever I spoke with them, especially when it involved discipline, I tried hard to project an authoritative tone, and I always tried my best not to speak with anger. Anger wasn't the answer, but the boys weren't angels, and there were times when their behavior really got to me, especially during their teens. Never once in their entire life did I, or Dad, ever *ridicule* any of the boys. Degrading them is the worst form of punishment. I learned that if I refrained from lashing out at them in a harsh tone, it was much easier for me to set a positive example. It wasn't easy, and I know they appreciated it.

There is no doubt in my mind that I made some mistakes along the way, but thanks to God, overall I was able to be both loving and firm in my dealings with them. They seemed to get the message and responded accordingly.

Chapter 24

Greetings from Uncle Sam

*I*n 1964, at the age of seventeen, Jack enrolled in Harbor Junior College. By 1966 he knew he'd be drafted into the Army, and without a word to anyone he enlisted in the Navy. The next day he asked Dad if the two of us could take him to Los Angeles because he'd enlisted in the Navy and he had to report for duty. In angry and disbelief I asked him why. "Because, Mom, the Army wants me and I don't want the Army." "But why now?" I protested. "You're still in school!"

This was the era of the Viet Nam War, with student unrest and civil rights riots in the cities. Young men between the ages of 18 and 25, who were not exempted for religious beliefs or who weren't students who received F1 classifications their names were entered in the draft lottery, and were randomly drawn to fill military vacancies. Towards the end of the conflict, it seemed like all the names were drawn. Registered students of colleges, universities, and recognized trade schools were automatically exempted. The student deferment at that time was F7, and I couldn't believe that Jack was walking away from this.

"Mom, I'm proud to be an American, and I can't escape my debt of service to our country. I'm not attracted to the Army, so my responsibility now is to serve the Navy. I owe at least three years of my life to Uncle Sam. Three years is nothing. Besides, I have a couple of weeks before I have to report for duty."

"Are we supposed to like your going now, at this time in your life?" I was terribly upset. Dad sat silently at the kitchen table, deep in thought. Jack Jr. was resolute. "Mom, you know what I have to do."

With our country in such turmoil, his enlistment really upset us. Jack Jr. and his brothers' lives were just beginning; I couldn't help but wonder what kind of a world they were going to live in. I constantly prayed, not only for our sons, but also for our society and the country we so dearly love.

On Sunday, October 2, 1966, Jack's girlfriend, Mimi, and all his friends gave him a going away party. The girls decorated our family room in a French motif: the Eiffel Tower was painted on one window, and a French table and chairs stood in the corner. Jack's friend Danny Hoeft supplied the music with his band and Gary Burrell and Dennis were waiters. All the furniture was pushed back to the wall to clear the dance floor. Dad and I led the dance while all the kids joined in. It was a great party, as everyone bid Jack goodbye and wished him God speed before they left.

At the appointed time the three of us headed for Los Angeles. Before we left, Jack turned his cherished red Impala over to his brother Patrick. "Take good care of it until I return." Patrick simply nodded, shook his hand, and wished his brother God speed. The trip to L.A. was very quiet. On arrival we said our good byes and waited for three hours at the recruiting station; then a Navy bus pulled up to take all those eighteen-and nineteen-year-olds to San Diego. We stayed until the bus was out of sight.

Facing the bitter truth that our son was on that bus, and God only knows where from there, made my heart ache. My stomach was churning and I fought to keep calm. In my mind I saw Jackie when he was a baby, learning how to walk. And now he was going off to war. Dad held my hand as the tears ran down my cheeks. Finally, he put his arm around me and started the car. As we drove home, he said, "We must put our faith in God."

Jack was at Harbor College for two years, but when he didn't start his third year in September he lost his F7 student deferment. He soon received his "greetings from Uncle Sam" ordering him to report to an induction center for processing. (I should've been reading his mail!) Fortunately he was in the reserves, but waited three months for school openings in the Navy. He only missed one question on their battery of tests. He was stationed at Treasure Island Naval Station in San Francisco and was allowed to come home on weekends. During which time he informed us that a motorcycle would be to his advantage while he was in school and the Navy would allow him to transport the motorcycle to his next duty station once school was completed. I was not overjoyed about a motorcycle for transportation, but I wanted to make it easy for him so, a Honda Motorcycle became his mode of transportation and we got to see more of him before he was transferred overseas. Dad did not like the idea of a motorcycle either.

Upon completing his Navy training he was sent to Northwest Cape in Exmouth, Australia, and eventually on to the USS *Forestall*. Jack remained in the service for six years. His superiors asked him to make a career out of the Navy, but he was anxious to return to the States and was honorably discharged on December 12, 1972

When Jack left there was no doubt in my mind that Patrick would be next. I tried to prepare myself, but it all seemed so unreal. Why did these young boys have to leave home to fight for something they're not responsible for? I was so upset, and not ready to accept what was in store for them.

Patrick entered Harbor College in 1967, and by September he was facing the draft and made the same choice as his older brother. Jack apparently had set the precedent. When Pat told us that he'd enlisted my heart sank. There was no need for me to remind him of his youth; it wasn't mine to reason why, not again! He knew how Dad and I felt. We drove him to L.A. and for the second time said our heartfelt goodbyes at the Navy recruitment center.

As I watched the bus disappear, the emptiness that came over me frightened me. Back in the car I said to Dad, "It isn't fair that we raise our boys only to send them off to war! I don't mean to sound unpatriotic, because I love my country, but I love these boys so much. Who's next?" My heart was breaking. Dad tried to comfort me, but I could see the stress in his face. I was so busy feeling sorry for myself that I'd paid little attention to how this was affecting him. I moved closer, put my head on his shoulder and my arm around his waist, and asked if he was OK. He looked down, put his arm around me, and with a smile at the corner of his mouth said, "I'm fine. We need to thank God for these boys and ask him to keep them safe." I said, "I pray for them all the time, honey." "I know you do. So do I, I just hope our prayers are enough."

In 1968 Terry entered Harbor College. After two years, he was at a crossroad in life and decided a college education could do him no good under the circumstances. He decided not to enroll the next semester. But his lottery number was ridiculously low and Uncle Sam had already snapped up all those with the same number. It was no good starting something else when Uncle Sam's greeting could show up at any time. So he signed up for a two-year hitch in the Army. History seemed to be repeating itself.

In 1970 we drove Terry to the recruiting station in L.A. and again watched the bus disappear. Dad sighed heavily. "Are you getting use to this routine, honey? There go three of our boys now, and you were right before—it's not fair." We learned later that Terry was bussed to basic combat training at Fort Ord, California. Later, during his training we were allowed to visit him.

When we arrived home, I tried to keep busy. Michael came to me and said, "Mom, try not to worry about the boys. I know it's not easy for you and Dad. I'm here if you need me." "Thanks honey," I said gratefully. "Prayers are powerful and we need to say a lot of them."

Michael's draft lottery number was very high and it didn't look as though he'd have to enlist. He was at California State University at Dominguez Hills, preparing to study law. Dennis's number was even higher than Michael's, so it seemed that there was no chance of his having to enlist. During the summer Dennis drove a delivery truck for Coca-Cola, then again in 1975 he drove a truck for a Stainless Steel Fabrication Company in Brooklyn, N. Y. biding his time before he entered the University of Southern California in preparation for his chosen career, Pediatric Dentistry.

The Navy allowed Jack to return home for Patrick's graduation from boot camp in San Diego. The enlisted men marched in front of the grandstand with the flag in full array. Everybody stood to salute the flag as the Navy band played "The Star Spangled Banner." Dad and I watched Jack salute our flag with great pride, standing perfectly erect in his white uniform. It was a breathtaking moment for both of us. Dad threw his shoulders back in an identical stance saluting the flag. I was so proud and emotional as I watched my two men with my right hand over my heart and tears in my eyes. It was such a momentous time in our lives. Later I was able to take a picture of both boys in their whites. It is time to sit down and give thanks for all that was so good with our family. Five great boys, what more can I ask.

The Navy prohibits brothers from duty on the same ship. Jack served on the *USS Forestall*, Patrick on the *USS Lucid*. They kept in constant touch with each other and wrote home on a regular basis. They were allowed to come home on holidays and we were grateful for every minute they could spend with us. Their Military checks were sent directly to me and I deposited them every month in their personal bank accounts. In time these funds were really appreciated.

During leave the boys started to make their true confessions. My sons had sufficient character to never do anything truly bad, but they got into their share of mischief. When they lived under my roof I was so close to them that I thought I'd done a perfect job in teaching them about right and wrong. But after they'd moved away they began to confess their mischievous deeds through the years. I honestly wanted to believe they were making up some of the stories they told me. And they were right under my nose all the time.

When Jack was home on leave, we had a conversation about the growing pains of his youth. I expressed my appreciation for his contribution to all of us, especially his guidance of his brothers. I told him I never had to worry about him or his younger brothers. What he said surprised me. "Mom, all those years, you really didn't expect us to sprout wings, did you? Some of the kids we were exposed to were not disciplined and sometimes they were hard to deal with. How were we supposed to handle certain situations if we didn't understand them firsthand? Our lifestyle for so many years was the greatest example we could've ever had, and it was set by you and Dad! You both cared about our friends, and us and best of all, you loved each other. We knew there was a good life out there if we wanted it. I know, *Dad said so.*" He said that with a slight grin as he looked down on me.

"Jackie, I hardly know what to say. I knew about certain things and we did have conferences about them, but I guess what I knew was just a drop in the bucket."

"Security was the answer, Mom. There were kids out there, who had no idea where they were going, had no goals. There were some things we just had to figure it out for ourselves. Our friends loved coming over here. They loved the way you and Dad treated them. They loved it when Dad played football with them, and they loved all those pep talks. It helped us all to help each other. It was guidance that we all needed. And Dad supplied that for us."

Then he added, "Terry took a liking to beer." "I know," I said, "but Dad got on his case big time. Terry thought he knew it all, but Dad knew how to handle him!" Well I think he did?

"That's right. That was his friend egging him on, but he was working with them in his own way and he was having fun at the same time. Fortunately, he knew how far to go with the beer, and he knew when to stop. I'm not sure he really liked the beer; I believe he just wanted to act sociable with his friends, that's my guess."

I nodded. "He really 'came to life' when he was sixteen, didn't he? I remember the time he was out late one Saturday evening with his friends, and he called me stating he did not have a ride home. They'd all been drinking, and his friend who was driving was two sheets to the wind. Terry knew he couldn't drive safely, so he took the car keys and threw them away. Dad was gone so he called me to pick him up. I was grateful for that. I really believe the beer was a passing fancy Jack, because I do not remember his drinking very much after that." "It's possible Mom. Only Terry can answer that." There were times (very few times) when I would get angry with Terry and the only way to get his attention would be for me to yell *"Marcus Aurelius."* Then Terry would look up and say, "OH-OH."

"How about Dennis, Mom? Has he told you about the problems he had at Miraleste? You know, Dennis could keep his cool in the most difficult situations. He just amazed me. He knew how to reflect sunny moods even when he wasn't feeling good and he was able to pass that mood on to others. He took no guff from anyone, and he stood his ground. He attracted the good guys, and he made some great friends. His attitude will take him a long way. You'll never have to worry about him; he has a good head on his shoulders."

I knew he was right. Dennis had worked hard at Miraleste High School, and the responsibility he'd had, as manager of the school store was good experience for him. He'd interview classmates to work different shifts at the store when he wasn't there, and that

192

kept him busy. He loved it, and he was proud of the new manager he appointed when he graduated.

"Angels we were not, but good sensible kids, yes! I'm proud of that, Mom!" "You're right, Jack, and I'm proud of that too."

I always felt good about allowing the boys to have space. There were times when they needed it. It wasn't easy for me especially when I felt I could be their best advisor. Dad and I had our own special conferences about this. The rule at all times was to be true to yourself, honest, and forthright in all they aspire to do. As long as they understood the importance of this rule, they would have little or no problem.

At the dinner table many times the boys would concoct outrageous stories about the day at school, and I'd listen in disbelief. Once they got me going, they kept embellishing the story. "I can't believe this," I'd protest. Finally I'd detect a slight grin on somebody's face, and then I'd stand up and shout, "Shame on you boys! How could you tell me such garbage? God is going to punish you." They'd all start laughing. "We really had you going, Mom!" They loved to tease me—and still do!

Terry's return from the service gave us a chance to reminisce as well. He surprised me with a story about kindergarten at Chester Rowell. (The school no longer exists.)

"Mom, you always bragged about how good I was, but I was a brat. I got mad at a little girl in my class one day. We were arguing at recess and I'm not sure why, but I grabbed her arms and swung her around in a circle, pretty fast, too. I let go and she fell to the ground in a puddle of mud. She screamed, as the teacher came over, "It's Terry's fault!". The teacher picked her up and sent me to the principal's office. The principal questioned me as to why I did that and my answer didn't please him, so he pulled me across his lap and gave me one hard slap on my impressive constitution. It really hurt, and I cried. The principal sent me back to class and told me if I ever did that again he'd report me to my parents."

I guess the expression on my face was a mixture of astonishment, curiosity and disappointment. When I tried to question him he said, "Oh, Mom, it was only kindergarten and I was a brat at school, but when I came home I was fine again." But Terry, I said, "The school never did call me." "That's right," he said. "I was only five years old and I never did that again. I did feel bad about it later, but I believe I was jealous of that little girl. I'm not sure why! The principal had a right to smack me; I deserved it!" I was too ashamed to tell you about it.

"Is there anything else you want to tell me?" "I can't think of anything at the moment." The slight grin in the corner of his mouth told me to leave it alone. Maybe I don't want to know everything.

One Sunday morning May 1970 I was alone in the house when the doorbell rang. As I passed the bay window I looked to see who was at the door. I saw someone in a U.S. Marines uniform standing tall with his back to the window. As I opened the door he turned around and with a big grin on his face he snapped to attention. Right away I recognized the boys' teen-age friend and our neighbor who lived around the corner. "Mike, look at you! You're beautiful!" I told him that I was happy to see him, and explained that the boys were all gone. "Yes, I know. I just wanted to talk to you before I return to the base."

I invited him in and he headed straight for the game table where he'd sat with our boys on so many occasions over the years. He looked so handsome in his uniform, so grown up and confident. We both sat down, and I'll never forget what he said to me.

"I wanted to come over to thank you and Mr. Nutter for having such wonderful sons. If it was not for them, I'd be on the inside looking out—you know, jail, big-time. That thought really scared me. It took time, but it was your sons who beat on me constantly. I was close to impossible to deal with, but they never gave up on me. I finally decided that if I were going to keep them as friends, I'd have to join them. We really went round and round many times over the years. I'm grateful for their friendship and I wanted you and Mr. Nutter to know how I felt. Those guys are the greatest. This is such a great family."

I thanked Mike sincerely and promised to tell Jack when he returned; adding that I knew Jack would be sorry he'd missed him. We both waved as he drove off and I stood there for a long moment, savoring the pride I felt in my sons and in this fine young man who had worked so hard to turn his life around. Mike did not know it at the time but it was me who was ready to give up on him.

In 1972 shortly after Jack's discharge from the Navy, the two of us were having breakfast together. Out of the clear blue sky he asked me if I would like to go riding. "Riding you say? Do you mean on your bike?" "Yes Mom, I would like to drive up the coast along the beach. What do you think?" "I don't think so Jack." "Oh, come on Mom, it will be fun." "I suppose it would be interesting and I do have a free day. OK. Jack, let me change my clothes!"

Leaving the gates of Rolling Hills I felt it best to bury my head in Jack's back. As he drove around dead mans curve (a dangerous section on PV Drive East) a car driven by a teenager shot out of his driveway without stopping right into Jack's path. Jack applied his brakes with such force; it was a miracle we did not end up all over the asphalt. At the signal below, Jack managed to catch up with the car and immediately jumped off the bike to talk to that teenager, but the kid managed to lock his door, stepped on the gas and shot out into the cross street of P. V. Drive North. Jack was so angry with him.

It was a thrill to ride on the back of his Kawasaki and I was proud of myself. This was my first ride on a motorcycle. I listened to the thrust of the bike's engine and I could feel the wind blowing against my face. Riding up the coast and on to Santa Monica was beautiful. We stopped for lunch and proceeded to tour what ever came along before returning home. Believe it or not, I rather enjoyed the ride.

The next morning Jack says, "Mom how would you like to maneuver the bike yourself?" "Me, no Jack, I would not." "Come on Mom. You would be the envy of the neighbors as you drive down Chuckwagon." "No, Jack they would think I am crazy." "I'm a good teacher Mom. OK, believe me, your going to love it."

Naturally he talked me into trying. Sitting high on his Kawasaki 500 Jack proceeded to explain its function. There are two things to remember. "First this is the ignition, (throttle) and this is the brake. Your right foot controls the brake; as does your right hand determines the speed. You turn the throttle slightly in order to get the feel of the bike. As you rotate a little more the bike speeds up. Keep that in mind he said? So let's practice." For about ten minutes, brake, throttle was all I did. It seemed easy enough. Then he turns the key; I feel the vibration and the bike and it is ready to go. It really surprised me, but as he was talking I accidentally turned the throttle full force. The bike kicked into gear and leaped into the air jerking me backward. Instead of letting up on my right hand I was hanging on to the throttle. I am headed for an empty field while Jack is screaming "brake, brake." Finally I started to apply the brake as Jack caught up to me. He reached over several times to kill the switch but in my shock I kept turning the handle bar and the bike would lunge forward with such force. Finally he was able to reach the switch and the bike was dead. I was so upset. Why I didn't go over the handlebars I'll never know. My son was furious with me!

I jumped off the bike and headed for the house. "Come back here Mom. I do not want you to be afraid of this bike." "Come back." "No." I said and entered the house. I proceeded to set at the kitchen table holding my head with both hands. I ask myself. "Why do I let these boys talk me into these things? After all these years, I still have not learned my lesson" Jack enters and is sitting beside me. "You know now what not to do, right? You need to try again. This is just an experience for you." "Jack, if I ever board that bike again, it will be because you are at the helm." "Please Mom, one more try." "No a thousand times no." Jack said, as he was leaving the kitchen table Mom I do not know what to do with you."" I felt bad because I know I frightened him. He tried so hard to get me to try again, but soon realized there was no deal. Not again. Have I learned my lesson this time? Yes I believe I have! Well we shall see! These boys are tricky you know!

Jack was allowed to attend Patrick's Boot Camp Graduation in San Diego, California 1976

Terry and Mom at Fort Ord, California 1971 Just before he was shipped to Viet Nam

**Jack Jr. grew a Beard
and Mustache
While in Asmara,
Ethiopia 1971**

**Jack Nutter
Home from the Navy
1973**

The Year 1968

Taken at the Beverly Hilton Hotel
in
Beverly Hills California
Nineteen Hundred Sixty Eight

Mary and Joseph League
Mardi Gras
Bal Magnifique

From Left to Right

Michael G. Nutter 18, Patrick J. Nutter 20,
Rachel E. Nutter (mom) 43, Jack W. Nutter Jr. 21, Jack W. Nutter Sr. (dad) 45
Dennis P. Nutter 16 and Terry M. Nutter 19

Chapter 25

Dad—First, Last, and Always

*J*ack Wilcox Nutter was the second of three boys born in Concordia, Kansas in 1923. His father, McKinley and his mother, Doris Nutter, were wheat farmers. Jack was an "A" student all through school, number one in all his classes. He worked the farm periodically after school with his two brothers and his father. Jack attended Kansas University, but was inducted into the Army after he had come down with scarlet fever and was too sick to enroll for the next semester. World War II was on the agenda and as his active duty status progressed and he was sent to Europe.

Jack had impeccable taste. He was always well dressed in a suit with a tie to match. He hated shopping, so I had all his suits made especially for him. In the morning when he was ready to leave for work, he was so handsome. I told him that he looked as though he just stepped off the cover of a magazine. He would smile, then he would lean over to kiss me good-bye. "Thank you, Mrs. Nutter." He had a deep heavy voice, which gave telephone callers the impression he was tall in stature. Actually he was only Five Feet, Seven Inches tall.

He quite often complimented workers and friends, but found it difficult to accept a compliment himself. He never looked down on anybody. He never lost his sense of humor and could communicate with anyone. He was good to everybody and everyone he met liked and respected him. He greeted almost everyone he passed in the street, elevator, or restaurant. He loved his work and the company he worked for. His work force always came first. Golf was one of his favorite sports, and he and the boys spent time on the golf course every chance they could.

While the boys were growing up, my work with them was endless. But during all these years, there was never a day when I had to pick up Jack's clothes or tidy up after him. He never created work for me with his personal effects. When I questioned him about this he said, "You have enough to do with the boys; you don't need for me to make more work for you!" I was elated—his concern really impressed me!

My love and devotion to him were complete. Our love for each other was the key to raising our sons. When he was troubled I comforted him. I'd clown around with crazy dance steps, and then I would tap him on the shoulder and "knight" him king of the Nutter household. That would bring a grin to his lips and he'd say, "Thank you, Mrs. Nutter, *you just made my day.*"

When I needed him he brought me complete joy. Only he knew how to raise my spirits. Always a compliment about anything and everything he knew about me. He told me how lucky he was to have met me, and how lucky we were to have such beautiful sons. He was so clever. He **never closed his eyes at night** without saying, "***I love you, Mrs. Nutter.***" As I'd reach over to hug him I'd echo his affection, and this <u>went on for years</u>.

When we shopped together Jack never paid for anything; he always entrusted me to handle the cash expenses, and proudly told those waiting on us that his "little bride" would take care of it. One day we were shopping for pajamas and small items for all the boys in my favorite Bullock Department store, (That department store no longer exists today) the clerk asked Jack how he wanted to pay. He pointed to me and said, "That's my little bride, and she has all the money." When the confused clerk asked how long we'd been married, I replied, "Oh, he always calls me his little bride. A bride I am not; we have five sons at home!"

Early in the boys' lives, Jack bought me a desk-model Necchi sewing machine. I used it to make the boys' white school uniform shirts, most of my own clothes and everything I could sew to save us money. Jack was proud of the things that came out of that machine, but he felt that I deserved more. His consideration of my needs always made me feel special. He would find reasons to shop and bring me some of the most beautiful outfits that he thought suited me best. When I asked him how he knew my size, he proudly said, "I told the clerk that I could put my arm around your waist and put my hand in my pocket! She said, 'Oh, size 10!'" We both laughed, but it worked for him.

One of Jack's customers, Mr. Armstrong, once invited us to a banquet for the loyal employees of his all-night restaurant in Fresno. During the evening Mr. Armstrong, whom Jack called Ernie, approached me and said, "I want to congratulate you, Mrs. Nutter." "Oh?" "Yes, I want to congratulate you for having such a wonderful husband." His words moved me and I replied, "Thank you; *he is special.*" "Very special, take it from me, I know." We chatted a few minutes and he had nothing but praise for Jack. This was only one of many compliments that I received about my husband over the years. They always made me ever so proud of him. When I would tell Jack about the compliments I would receive, he would melt. He would give me a long "R e a l l y." He never felt he was special. He was just plain Jack to himself, but not to me.

During one of our business trips to Chicago back in1956, Jack and I attended an employee awards banquet for his company. We were seated at a large round table, and eventually joined by eight other gentlemen from all over the country. Jack introduced the both of us to each of the men as they arrived. During the next two hours we had dinner and Jack chatted casually with each man as we watched the awards presentation.

As Jack and I bid goodnight to our fellow guests, Jack addressed each of the eight men by his full name, and made reference to each man's remarks during the evening. The last man he spoke to said to Jack, "We all met here tonight for the first time, yet you addressed each of us by our full name and even remembered our dinner conversations. I am so impressed. *I take my hat off to you, sir.*" All the other gentlemen nodded and smiled.

Returning to our room, I told Jack that I too was very impressed by his remarkable memory. I asked him how he managed to remember not only eight strangers' full names and job titles, but also details of their personal lives in their casual conversations that evening. He looked at me with that lopsided grin of his and said, "By association, honey. I find something about the person that I can connect to their name, and it doesn't leave my mind. You should work on this too, because you meet so many people with all your club work and activities. It is good exercise for the brain!" "That's easy for you to say, but not for me to do!" I replied with a smile. But "OK, I will work on it honey."

Early in Jack's career, Leggett and Myers supplied an eight-by-eleven calendar to their customers for the **Christmas Holiday.** It was a beautiful bright red cover with large broad white letters of "Pall Mall" across the front. Jack brought it home and as he flipped the pages to show me the big squares he said, "Do you think you can use this honey? As I looked it over I said, "What a great calendar, honey I love it honey?". You mean I can have it." "Yes" "Ok consider it mine."

In January the following year I started marking the squares in the calendar on the days he was absent for our evening ritual. He was good about calling, so I was able to note in the square where he was the evening in question. It is important to know why and where he spends his time in the evenings. In order to place any piece of equipment in any one location like restaurants, bars, hotels and the like, it was vital that he see the manager or the owner of the establishment. Therefore, he might make several calls to one location before he could accomplish his goal. As it turned out, most of the time his contacts had to take place in the evening and essentially more than one visit. Unfortunately his clients always came first. For me, it was a nightmare, but I made myself understand.

I crossed each square from corner to corner of that calendar indicating his absence, with an insertion of where he was that night. It was obvious the plain squares on each month meant he honored us with his presence at the dinner table that evening. I faithfully did this for a full year. At Christmas that year I presented that calendar to him as a gift. I will never forget the expression on his face as he scanned the pages. Astonished by what I had done, he looked at me and said, *"Is this a record of my evening activity, All Year?"* I shook my head yes. *"I know this is true, as he continued to scan, but I cannot believe my lack of concern for you. This is not fair to you honey. I need to change my habits, don't I?"* Again I shook my head. He hugged me and said I was going to love the new Jack Nutter. You're going to get tired of me." "Never." Well, he was good for about two weeks and without realizing it, he was sinking back in to his old tricks again. I knew he was not going to change, the demands of his business meant too much to him, so I simply had to accept him the way he was.

But it was a great two weeks. The little boys occupied so much of my time in his absence, what else could I do. I wanted him home all the time, but I could not allow myself to make both his life, and mine, miserable by insisting on it. I took what I could get and I was happy when we were together. He always tried to make up the difference with some of his outlandish gifts. One time he bought me a portable TV that I could set on top of the sink in the kitchen. I could work and watch TV at the same time. Wouldn't you know he would think of that? He still wanted to keep me busy. I loved that little TV and I loved his thoughtfulness.

Not many things would "leave" Jack's mind. Many was the time he'd be reading the newspaper while I would tell him about the boys' activities that day, and I'd be sure he never heard a word I said. Then, about an hour later, he would comment on my story, or answer my question, and I'd have to ask him what in the world he was talking about. He'd lower his paper, look at me quizzically, and say, "Well, didn't you tell me?" Then quote me word for word! I'd reply, "But I told you that over an hour ago!" And his response would be, "There's a little box in the back of my head, and when I'm busy, everything else sits in there until I can get to it. "You know what honey, I said, I really believe you. No wonder I can never get a straight answer out of you."

Jack encouraged me to make notes about the little things the boys did over the years, so I entered memorable events in a binder. "And date them," he'd say to me. "When our sons get older they're going to love reading your notes. And don't forget that incident when Jack and Patrick hosed Grandpa's gas tank. That'll frost them later!" He simply swept me off my feet with his enthusiasm and his confidence in me, but as he requested I started making short notes.

The gas tank incident occurred one summer when the boys were preschoolers. Grandpa Nutter and his wife, Emma, had just arrived for a visit after driving all the way from Concordia, Kansas. As he got out of his car Grandpa yelled out to Dad, "My tank is just about empty, Jack; perhaps I should go to the station before I forget." "Oh, let it be," Dad said. "Come in for a visit first and we'll go later." "OK," said Grandpa, but before taking his place in the house he stopped to greet Jackie and Patrick, who'd come out to welcome him.

Later that day Grandpa couldn't start his car. "What's going on here?" he said, as he cranked the engine. I know there was enough gas to get me to the station." The two little angels ran and hid. Dad, suspicious, went looking for them. He grabbed them by the back of their shirts and demanded, "Why is Grandpa having so much trouble with his car? What have you boys done?" Jackie looked up and said, "We wanted to help Grandpa, so we took the hose and filled his tank with water." **"WATER?"** Jack howled. "I don't believe this! Get in the house!" Time, energy, and money meant nothing to those boys at that age—but they never did it again. Poor Grandpa!

Grandpa loved the Santa Anita Horse Races. He always made it a point to venture to California during racing season. His money was burning a hole in his pocket and Dad's work schedule made it impossible for him to attend the races with him. So guess who was elected to take Gramps and Emma. I knew nothing about horses or betting but it didn't take me long to learn. I had some anxious moments as I watched my horse run down the track, with my money pinned to his back. Most of the time it was money down the drain. Gramps felt that Bill Shoemaker was the greatest jockey that ever lived and invariably he would bet on Shoe and not the horse. Who ever won that day was elected to buy dinner for all before returning home. Poor Gramps! Those were fun days and it made Jack happy to know that his father was being entertained.

Late one afternoon Jack asked me how I would like to take a drive to Canada for a couple of weeks. It seems that his busy routine at the office was getting to him and he needed to get away. "How about the little boys honey?" "No boys, not this trip." I always hated leaving our boys but at the same time I was excited that he wanted to go and naturally I made the necessary arrangements. We had a 16 mm movie camera and it was time to put it to good use.

This was 1957 and we considered this as our first real vacation; we felt like newlyweds. The 101 highways along the coast were slow but very interesting until we crossed into Victoria. The drive into Canada was so beautiful. We spent time at beautiful Bush Gardens filming its beauty of the hundreds of flower varieties. Jack spoke to a gentleman who was caring for the grounds.

This man was so interesting explaining the care and love for the different plants. Jack was so fascinated.

We then boarded a Ferry for a picturesque cruise through the Gulf Islands and on to beautiful Vancouver. Before checking into the Waterfront Hotel we drove through a couple of parks including Queen Elizabeth Park. I was enthralled. Our stay at the hotel was so beautiful; Jack found himself enjoying every aspect of this hotel and it's surrounding. Naturally my thoughts kept going back to Fresno, so we spent time in Canada's distinctive Gift Shops making different purchases for the boys. What a trip!

Arriving home we found Terry sitting on the garage roof pulling the singles off and throwing them in the driveway. When he saw us he quickly scrambled down the ladder and on to the driveway. When I questioned him about this he said, "I asked the babysitter if it was OK to do this and she said it was OK with her." "Terry aren't you ashamed of yourself? What a terrible question for you to ask this lady when you knew better! Right?" "Yes." "You were being destructive and I am so ashamed of you." He would not look up at me. "I'm not going to punish you this time Terry, but I can tell you if you try anything like this again you will have to take double punishment. Right now I want you to go out to the driveway and gather all those singles before something happens to them." He looked up and said he was sorry. Mrs. Syvertsen happened to be out of town at the time we left so we hired another sitter who came to us highly recommended. We never hired her again.

In all the years we were married Jack never forgot my birthday or our anniversary. On our twelfth anniversary, April 6, 1958 he sent flowers to our favorite restaurant and he had Champagne sitting on the table when we arrived. I was so impressed with his thoughtfulness and his endearing words of love that it over powered my feelings. Trying to please him I got carried away with the Champagne. Before he realized what was happening he found himself helping me to the car with only bubbles swarming in my head and no food in my stomach. He went to so much work and I ruined our evening. Mrs. Syvertsen and the little boys wondered why we were home so early. Jack said, "Oh Mom doesn't feel very good but she will be OK." I apologized the next morning with a promise I would never do that again. He hugged me and said, "We will celebrate tonight here at home without Champagne." "That's great honey and thanks for the beautiful flowers, the cake the Champagne and especially your understanding, I really feel bad." With a smile he said. "No more Champagne for you." "Your right honey it was great but I just cannot take the liquid refreshment. You're not angry with me are you?" As he hugged me he said "No a thousand times no." "Thank you honey."

January 1960 Jack was gone for three weeks with the new Oklahoma subsidiary. A couple of days before returning home he called me and asked if I could arrange a three-day get-a-way trip for just the two of us. I questioned his request and he explained the work had been such a drain on him that he wanted to spend three days strictly R and R. before returning to work. (Rest and Recuperation) Besides honey, you need a rest from the boys. I had just gotten over a bad cold and he was right I needed time off." Any place special." I asked? "Yes he said, how about the Beverly Hilton in L.A.?" I told him it was no sooner said then done. I called Mrs. Syvertsen making sure she was available. I called the Hilton for reservations and then I picked him up at the Los Angeles International Air Port and we drove directly to the Hilton. He was so happy simply sitting around the pool and doing nothing. We casually dressed for dinner and had breakfast brought to our room. We played cards and, of course, he practiced his card tricks on me. Essentially we enjoyed each other's company. No work schedule is what intrigued me most. A great deal of our conversation was about the boys and I naturally found little gifts to bring home to them. It was one of the greatest three days the two of us ever had. We should have done it more often.

During the years Jack and I were married the two of us were responsible in voting for three presidents of our choice into the White House. When Dwight D. Eisenhower appeared on the ballot, my concerned husband one evening after everything was quiet on the home front; took me by the hand and told me we needed to talk. "About what, I asked?" As he fumbled with a few words I said, "What's on your mind honey?" "Well, you know we are about to go to the polls to vote for the man of our choice." "Right." "I guess what I want to know, and you don't have to tell me if you don't want to, but I just want to be sure you are not going to cancel out my vote." "Is that all?" I reached over hugged him, and I put his mind to rest by saying, "you haven't a worry in the world."

He had a grin on his face a mile long, and said, "How about I take you out for dinner tonight?" "No honey, I have dinner in the oven. But I will take you up on it later." See how easy it is to make your husband happy.

September 1965 Jack and I ventured to Dodger Stadium to see the world's greatest pitcher in baseball. I hated baseball, but Jack said I would learn to love it by the time this game was over. Sandy Koufax a left-handed pitcher was phenomenal that day. In the city of the Angeles, Los Angeles, California, Jack and I watched Koufax in awe; as did his teammates and a crowd of 29,000 see the only pitcher in baseball history to hurl four no-hit, no-run games. He had done it four straight years in a row. The game meant very little to me, but Jack was good at explaining the games function as we went along. The crowd was going wild and Jack would jump up and down as we hugged each other. My husband who was always so well disciplined in public went as wild as everyone. At one point he grabbed my head with both hands, pulled his nose to mine and yelled, "Nowwww what do you think of base ball?" I screamed, "I love it." In our embrace we saw the sky as it rained Dodger blue seat cushions cascading down from the upper reaches of Heaven. Koufax surrounded by these cushions just stood there right in front of us bowing ever so often. I was so enthralled and privileged to be one of those 29,000 fans. Vince Scully allowed the crowd to cheer as we all watched teammates leap into Koufax's arms. If only I could have had a camera with me. Then he disappeared into the dugout. Summoned for a curtain call, he came out, tipped his cap, and disappeared again. The following year Koufax retired at age thirty. No other sports hero had retired so young, and so completely. It was history in the making and we were part of it. His left arm was so full of arthritis he could not straighten it anymore. My heart ached for him.

One Saturday morning Jack and Dennis decided to go shopping and they asked me if I would like to go with them. "Look at me honey, I'm not appropriately dressed." "Oh your fine Mom, he put his arm around me and said let's go." Del Amo shopping center in Torrance California sported my favorite Broadway Department Store. (Today it no longer exists.) Upon arrival we decided to part. "Let's meet back here in an hour". "OK Mom?" "Sure". The boys went upstairs to the men's department. I browsed through handbags and saw one I liked, but it was locked in the glass counter. I summoned a clerk for help. I pointed to the purse and said, "May I see this purse please?" As she looked down her nose at me, she sarcastically said, "We have many bags in the store, but this one is much too expensive and you would not be able to pay for it. You may look further if you wish." "No thanks." I was so embarrassed and shocked I bowed my head and walked away.

Dad and Dennis finally made their appearance and Jack knew immediately something was wrong. When I related my experience he said, "Show me the purse and the clerk." No, honey it's too embarrassing." I told you I should not have come. He insisted. I pointed to the purse and the clerk. Jack summoned the clerk over and he said, "My wife was here earlier and you insulted her. For your information my wife can buy and sell you many times over. As he pointed to the bag, may we see this one please?" She nervously produced the bag. "You like this honey?" "No not now." As he checked the tag he reached for his money clip that was thick with one hundred dollar bills and assured the clerk we wanted it. After producing his receipt and change he said harshly. "It is not your duty to prejudge those who shop at your counter. You insulted my wife today and you are a disgrace to this department store. If I were your employer I would fire you!" He put his arm around me and said, "Let's get out of here honey."

Our long awaited trip to Acapulco Mexico was a dream come true. Our reservation at the Las Brisas Hotel was a sight to behold. We were high above Acapulco Bay with such magnificent views. As we watched the moonlight hit the water from our balcony my husband held me in his arms and his eyes sparkled with incredulous amazement of this natural beauty. It was an impressive romantic getaway for the both of us. How I loved being with him. He would ask, "Are you happy honey?" My reply, "I'm always happy when I'm with you." As we looked out through our bay window, he would hug me from behind, and whisper sweet nothings in my ear. I would turn and face him straightaway, look directly in his eyes, and repeat my love for him. The endearing words that came out of his mouth always made me love him more as the years rolled by. He was so special!

We attended every activity available to us in Acapulco and dinned in their finest restaurants. We had continental breakfast delivered to our room each morning. During the day Jack rented a Jeep with a blue canvas awning to tour the city and we ventured into areas that Taxi's dare not go. At one point a Mexican Vender jumped in front of our Jeep fanning his bright orange Serape and Jack said, "Look honey, he thinks I'm a bull." We stopped to check his merchandise and Jack tried to visit with him a few minutes. It was strictly sign language for them. "Mom," he said, "how about we take this orange serape with black feet. You like it." "Ok with me." We thanked the vendor and bid him good-bye as we headed for the famous Mexican cliff divers from the La Perla Restaurant. To witness those divers as they flew into the air between those enormous cliffs and down into the ocean below was a sight to watch. Wow! We were so impressed.

Our future together was always taken for granted. He always felt that today is today and the future will take care of itself. He had no elusions of glory. He maintained that, "He works every day and brings home the bacon, while I work caring for the boys and running the household; what else is there?" I said, "Some day honey we are going to be senior citizens." He impatiently said, "Not tomorrow. Now let's go find a good restaurant I'm hungry." There were signs all over Mexico reading "No Tipping" that intrigued us. What a treat, and what a great trip!

The summer of 1967 the City of Rolling Hills was experiencing a devastating menace. Thousand of mice invaded our community and every household was affected. From the mouse that disappeared into the grout of the fireplace bricks *right before our eyes*; to the mouse who *died in the dish washer as I tried to drown him*; and to the mice we found *dead* under the family room couch as dad was reading his news paper and watching TV. I could go on and on.

Finally, in the middle of the night I heard a mouse drop in our *chrome wastebasket.* I tugged at Jack, "Wake up honey, a mouse just fell in the basket." He said, "Oh, please honey; it's your imagination, go to sleep." I buried my head under the blankets and in his back. Early the next morning Jack was shaking me. "Honey wake up, you were right last night, *a mouse did fall in the basket,* but don't worry, I will take care of it." "Oh Thanks Honey." Later at breakfast I glanced out our bay window and noticed the basket at our front door. In checking, the mouse was *still* in the basket running around in a circle. I closed the door and ignored it. He said he would take care of it, so be it.

Later that day, as Pat entered the front door he called out, "Mom, Did you see the mouse in the basket?" "Yes, I said, disgustingly." "Oh." Again, much later Dennis called me, "Mom did you see the mouse in the basket?" Again a long disgusted, "Yes." "Oh." At dinnertime as we were sitting at the table waiting for Dad and we noticed on his arrival, he hesitated at the front door. He came in, washed his hands, took his place at the table and said, "Fellows did you?" The boys interrupted him and said, "Yes dad, we saw that mouse in the basket." I said, "Dad, you are elected to say grace." He looked at me and said, "OK." After giving thanks he said, "And please dear God, do something about that mouse in the basket!" The boys bowed their heads with silly grins on their faces, but not another word was spoken.

Early the next morning I heard Jack in the kitchen talking to the boys. Something has got to be done about that poor little mouse in the basket. Jackie said, "Don't look at me." Terry said, "It's not my basket." I ignored the front door all day. As I was ready to retire that evening I noticed Jack glaring at me with a silly grin on his face as he was lying in bed. Every move I made his eyes followed me. I thought to myself, now what? I glanced down and saw the basket had been returned, *empty.* As I climbed into bed I crawled over to kiss my husband goodnight and he grabbed me and said, *"Are you happy now?"* We both laughed heartedly over that mouse in the basket, but not one word as to its demise! I couldn't have cared less.

During my term as president of the Mary and Joseph League in Palos Verde's, Jack presented me with my own personal white and gold gavel. He'd had it inscribed with the words "Rae Nutter, Mary and Joseph League, 1969–1970," so that I could call the meetings to order in style, he said! He was ever constant of my needs and I loved him for his thoughtfulness. From time to time I would find him sitting in the back of the room during one of my meetings, and later he would tell me that he had dropped by because he wanted to take me to lunch. During lunch he'd compliment me on the meeting and give me pointers for the next meeting. He was so thoughtful!

Once, while vacationing in Hawaii we were waiting at a bus stop, and I chatted with a very friendly lady there. Out of the clear blue sky she asked me, "What was it about your husband that made you want to marry him?" I thought that was a strange question, but never the less I looked over at Jack, who was sitting on a large rock nearby listening to us, and I said, "That's an easy question for me; I married my husband because he was *kind, thoughtful, and considerate.*" The lady responded, "Very interesting." Then Jack said, "Oh, shucks," snapped his fingers, and added, "I thought she was going to say it was because I was *handsome, sexy, and rich!*" We all roared with laughter as Jack proceeded to help us onto the approaching bus. He was so versatile in everything he said and did and he did it with ease, but he was never a show-off.

On one of our early trips to Hawaii Jack invited our friends Will and Isabelle Ayers as our guests. It was his way of saying thanks for their thoughtfulness to us over the years. Our treat would be their stay at the Hawaiian Village Hotel. (Later became Hiltons Hawaiian Village) Our friend the Feeney's accompanied the four of us on this trip as well. On our first day we all decided to spend time on Hawaii's beautiful beach. Jack had taken a deck of cards with him and the boys decided to play poker in the sand that afternoon. They rented a gigantic umbrella and the boys hovered under this umbrella for protection from Hawaii's sun as they played cards. Unfortunately without realizing it, Jack carelessly allowed his right foot to linger beyond the shade and into the sun. That night he was miserable. His foot was so swollen and painful. He was given antibiotic for pain and crutches in order to get around. So the first week we simply toured Oahu. We visited the Arizona Memorial and Battleship Missouri. We dinned At Diamond Head Hotel and shopped at the Ala Moana Shopping Mall. My favorite shopping place in the sun.

The second week Jack was back to walking so we all went island hopping. We flew to the Big Island, rented a car and drove all over the island. We visited one of the world's most active volcano and ending up at the Black-sands beach. I collected a jar of that sand and brought it home with me. (That jar is still in my

213

possession to this day.) Our next flight was on to beautiful Kauai where we stayed overnight. The men continually had poker fever with cards in one hand and a drink in the other hand. They were happy and we were having a ball in Hawaii's beautiful gift shops spending their hard earned money. We visited the famous Fern Grotto for the singing of the Hawaiian Wedding Song. That was so heart rendering and before leaving the islands Jack expressed his desire to visit the Polynesian Cultural Center. The six of us enjoyed the elaborate song and dance spectacle, which featured more than one hundred performers. It was an amazing and beautiful experience. I shall never forget it. Can you imagine how difficult it is to ease back to normal when you're having so much fun?

When the boys were dating they were always short of cash. They knew that Dad always carried enough cash in his pocket but they would say to the both of us, "Could I borrow a couple of dollars, Mom?" I'd say, "I don't have any cash, honey, how about you Dad?" Jack would reach for his money clip and as he did I would reach for a twenty, and he would yell, "Be careful, he only wants a couple!" I would say, "What can he do with a couple?" Who ever had asked for the money would say "Thanks, Mom, and you too Dad," as they vacated the house. I would yell, "Do we know where you're going?" "A movie, remember?" "OK, be home by twelve!"

Our work for the Mary and Joseph League in Los Angeles was gratifying to both of us. We were only two of the many people who assisted our beloved moderator, Sister Mary Ignatius, (God rest her soul) in presenting the Mardi Gras BAL Magnifique. In 1968 we were asked to reign as the *Grand Duke* and *Grand Duchess* of the Bal. That momentous evening was one of our proudest moments, as Jack placed my arm under his the two of us marched down the aisle to the music of our royal court. The entertainment for the evening festivities was Jan Murray and Jerry Lewis. It was an elegant time in our lives.

It is true the love of his life *first*, was his business; me, myself and I, rated *second* then our five sons came in *third*. He loved all the sports, and all the musicals that came along. He loved to Jitter Bug and I loved it when he led me to the dance floor. He loved to take close-up pictures of the boys with his miniature Minolta camera. He took endless movies with our 16mm movie camera. Above all he loved to frequent the boutique shops while he was out of town, for unusual attire for me. His taste for quality and style was unusual. I never wanted to return anything he purchased for me. He loved going to church with us and he was ever so generous with his donations to the church. When he asked me how much I was giving to the collection basket on Sunday, he would frown at my answer and say "don't be such a piker Mrs. Nutter."

The Arthur Murray Dance Studio quite often advertised "Specials." I answered to one of these specials and set up an appointment to try one of their classes. Jack was reluctant to go, but when I told him the first class was FREE he consented but he was not happy. At the studio that evening we were paired with different instructors and their simple little dance steps infuriated Jack. About fifteen minutes later we were returned to our husbands to proceed with music on what was taught to us. As the music began my husband pulled me across the dance floor and demonstrated his awesome style of dancing. I loved it and as the other students applauded us he took a slight bow. The instructor complimented us on our routine, but felt we were too advanced for the class. We were excused. Jack was not the least bit disappointed.

On Jack's forty fifth birthday I gave him a Surprise Party. The invitation specifically noted they arrive early and no gifts allowed. The food was catered with prime rib and all the trimmings; and a professional bar tender served drinks to our guests. When Jack walked in the front door his father was the first to greet him and he positively melted. His long time secretary from Fresno Vera and her husband Al, Ed and Margie Rodger, Emma Lines of Hawaii and Culver City top employees were the height of the party. He was at a complete loss for words but graciously greeted everyone individually.

Our many trips included Canada, Acapulco Mexico, Chicago, Santa Cruz, Las Vegas, Palm Springs, Monterey and San Francisco many times over. He loved dinning at the Torrington Restaurant on the Wharf in San Francisco. Our Hawaii trips four times a year we always stayed at our Ilikai Hotel. It became my home away from home. All these are filled with beautiful indestructible memories. It may be hard to believe, but we never fought about anything, we had many conferences, but we never spoke harsh words to each other. Our time together was so short; there was nothing worth fighting about. I hated his extensive traveling, but I made the best of it. Our five sons keep me constantly busy and we loved our travels together.

Just returned from dinner at Jacks favorite hide away the *Beverly Hilton Hotel.* **We were Celebrating his 45ᵗʰ 𝔅irthday with friends, family employees from 𝔉resno and ℭulver ℭity 𝔒ffice.**

The stars, Nat King Cole, Jerry Lewis, Dean Martin, Bob Hope, Bing Crosby, Don Ho, Elvis Presley, and Perry Como, how he loved them. Eleanor Powell's come back in Las Vegas was really special for him. The Frank Sinatra specials he never missed and the Dina Shore specials lifted his musical heart. When Theresa Brewer appeared on stage and belted out a song; her voice captured his heart. He loved listening to her and was the first to stand up and cheer as she graciously bowed to her audience. Watching the Tonight Show with Johnny Carson was one of my favorite programs. Since it was so late it gave me time to wait for Jack to arrive, and many times he came home early enough to watch the end of the show with me.

Many years later after the Vietnam War as our three son's homecoming from overseas duty was one of the happiest days of our lives. To be so lucky to have three boys return from the thick or the action safe and sound was a blessing from God. For that we shall be eternally grateful

Five weddings produced eighteen grandchildren in all. On one occasion as Jack held our first grandson in his arms, Rodney

Jack Nutter Jr., he looked at me and said, *"Remember these days, honey?"* In all the years that we were married, we had benefited beyond our wildest hopes and dreams from all that was good in our marriage. The continuity of life that bound us together made us the greatest family of our years. Under the circumstances we couldn't possibly have done any better.

We have been lucky enough to have most of our grandchildren living close by and we have spent some of our happiest hours with them. I loved it when I was asked to baby sit and I did a lot of baby-sitting in my day. But today, all those grandchildren are teenagers and no need for grandma's expertise.

THE MARY AND JOSEPH LEAGUE
PRESENTS THE
NINTH ANNUAL

Mardi Gras
Bal Magnifiquie

OF
GREATER LOS ANGELES

GRAND DUKE AND GRAND DUCHESS
Jack and Rachel Nutter

Music for Dancing
LES BROWN AND HIS BAND OF RENOWN

Beverly Hilton Hotel
February the Twenty Fourth
Nineteen Hundred Sixty-Eight

Chapter 26

Farewell to Dad

*I*n 1946, when Jack and I decided to get married, we had long conversations about our future together. We started off on a shoestring, but our material wealth grew alongside our love for each other as the years rolled by. We had our ups and downs, but we kept our love alive. Jack made the six of us happy and that is all that counted. What he wanted, I wanted for him, with never a question in my mind that we couldn't work things out.

Now comes the most stressing part of our lives. The difficulty and heartaches we both endured started at a very late time in our marriage. It was also a time when we should have realized our shortcomings, we should have been able to see the handwriting on the wall, put our pride aside, and search for some answers with professional help. The terrible mistakes we made because of both his and my pride devastated our marriage.

Marriage—the effort to bond two people together—is a delicate and fragile thing. Sometimes it works, and sometimes it fails. Nothing is perfect in life, especially in a marriage, and fairy-tale endings are for children's bedtime stories. Unfortunately, our marriage failed at a time of great stress, disappointment and pride starting with work.

For years Jack had focused his attention to the top of the ladder for success. He had always been a very determined individual; once he made up his mind about something, he pursued it to the end. He was fair, honest and true to everything he achieved in his business dealings. In Fresno he was called Honest Abe, and in Culver City he held a Vice President position and was admired and respected by all employees. His wit and humor only made us love him more as the years rolled by. His employers both Davre and Henry Davidson (God rest their souls) gave him unlimited responsibilities over the years. It takes time to be successful but in later years as time rolled by my husband became impatient and short with me; irritable and difficult to get along with; very unusual for such a proud and patient man! I thought it was the long hours at the office and the days spent away on business trips. I was never allowed to intervene with the business so I prayed for solicitude instead.

The trials and tribulations in raising teenagers can be devastating when one parent is on the move seventy five percent of the time. Our boys were not difficult; it was just that there were five directions being pursued. They were extremely well behaved (not angels) but all the same they needed guidance. As the sole responsibility rested on my shoulders, I began to pressure Jack for support. He was already undergoing company pressures and did not welcome my plea. In his mind I could handle any thing that came around concerning the boys. I did not need him. So he thought.

The most serious problems with the boys invariably took place while Jack was out of town. My central nervous system was taking a beating so I decided a part-time job would help me to get away from the initial problems. It worked out great for a while. During this time, Terry was playing football for his Hi School Football Team after school hours. During one of the practice games he fell in a twisted position as he was reaching for a pass and one of the other players fell on him. Results, spirals break on his left leg, which was tremendously painful. Eventually he was put on crutches which limited his ability to get around and that did not help his attitude, he was impatient at times but we worked it out. I could see that this part-time activity of mine was becoming a detriment and it had to go. Soon, Terry was back to normal again, and so was our household. Amen.

It wasn't long when my dearest friend Marion and my sister-in-law Connie introduced me to a bowling league. Our league started early in the morning and was over by one in the afternoon. It was fun and I looked forward to those days of relaxation and I was home before the boys returned from school. Unfortunately my independence and additional activities did not meet with Jack's approval. He would prefer that I stay home. After awhile, I finally came to the conclusion that fighting the inevitable was impossible. To keep my husband happy I needed to be where he wanted me. What else is there? I loved my independence, but it was not working well for me.

During this time Jack's employer was being honored with a surprise party in Honolulu Hawaii and all key employees and their wives were invited. Nothing could have pleased me more. On the plane that day Jack was cool and aloof. Arriving at our hotel in the early afternoon we checked in to our quarters and Jack immediately left for the office. I waited for him in the hopes we would have dinner together. Instead he accepted an invitation for dinner with other office guests leaving me to dine alone. That really hurt, but I said nothing. I have had to dine alone before so it did not leave an impact on me. He left early the next morning again only to present himself back at the hotel early enough to dress for the evening celebration. To be distant with me in the privacy of our living quarters and any time we were alone was very unusual. I felt that he was so preoccupied with business he simply forgot I was around. I hated it!

To greet everyone at the party and in the presence of company personnel he was, *as usual, charming and caring to my every need, holding my hand constantly.* No one was aware of the tension between the two of us, but in my mind I was given renewed hope with this affection. We have always had an infinite capacity to rejuvenate our feelings, we cared about each other and that was all that counted besides, it is not his nature to be thoughtless and inconsiderate. Arriving home Jack announced that he was leaving. Without my knowledge he had rented an apartment close to work before we left for Hawaii. "You're what?" I could not and would not believe him. As I unpacked his suitcase, he tried to convince me he truly was leaving by returning his clothes to his case. I said, "I cannot believe what you are saying to me. After all, we have five sons to take into consideration." "The boys will have to understand. I really want to be alone for a while. Give me some time to find myself and before you know it I will realize how much I love you and the boys, and I will return." "Find yourself? You've got to be kidding." My heart was beating like a drum!

I did not want to accept this, so I pleaded with him. "Please listen to me, honey. During our life together we both have had a sense of duty to each other, and in our zest for life we have acquired the love, respect, and admiration of almost every one around us. Please, honey; what we have here today took years to acquire. To walk out now *only* because you want to go it alone or because you want to find yourself sounds crazy. Now is the time for us to start doing for each other. Until the boys return, we are free. We have only each other to think about now. It can't get any better." I continued. "There is no one in this whole wide world that I ever want to share the rest of my life with. I do not want to share holidays with anyone but you and the boys. I love you, I need you honey, and I want you here with me as long as we both shall live! Isn't that the promise we made to each other when we said our marriage vows? Please honey; I do not want to be alone! Dear God, how have we managed all these happy years together?"

He said, "I have thought about all of this, but perhaps what I need is a good jolt. Let me try this for a while." "How long?" "I'm not sure, but I will keep in touch." Again I pleaded, "Jack, I'm not perfect, I have my faults, please tell me what I am doing wrong? Perhaps I am trying too hard, but tell me what to do that will make you happy. I can change." He became indignant. "You're doing it again; you nag, nag, nag, and it has gotten to the point that I don't look forward to coming home any more." "You're right, I do nag, but how can I help it when you are gone so much? Is it wrong because I want to see more of you? Answer me please! Honey what is it with you?" He then became totally out of control and said, "Let me go, I need time. I will call you." He was so distraught he picked up his suitcase and walked out the door. I realize that was not the time to let him go, but what could I have done to keep him home. Tie him to the chair. I wish!!!

I was stunned. This was not the man I had married, the man I had dedicated my life to. I was unable to think clearly. All the little things that I'd tried to ignore for so long were staring me in the face. I thought I would lose my mind, but I knew that I had to keep my wits about me, if for no other reason than for the sake of our sons.

On several occasions, Jack asked me to withdraw large sums of money from our savings, saying only that he needed it and I was not to concern myself about it. It made me unhappy, but what could I do at this point. I watched our sizeable nest egg that we both worked so hard to save for rainy days dwindle little by little and I worried about the ARA stock we had. I had to do something. I contacted our jeweler in Los Angeles and told Sam that Jack wanted to purchase a nice diamond ring for my birthday. He checked on his suppliers and found various diamond cuts, but when he found the raw Five Carat Diamond,—that was it! I made Sam think that Jack was out of town and between the two of us we could convert this diamond into a platinum setting. He customized the diamond by adding five, three fourth carat size, pear shape, diamonds. He arranged them so that they surrounded the five-carat in a half circle in an up-word position. It was beautiful.

I called Jack telling him that I had something important to show him and could we have lunch together. He picked me up at the house and drove to our favorite restaurant in Torrance. After ordering he said, "You had something to show me?" "I do." I reached for a Kleenex in my purse and slowly uncovered this beautiful brilliant ring, then placed it on my finger. He was so surprised he ran his fingers through his short hair as his eyes glared at the diamond. He gave a big heavy sigh, and I knew this ring bothered him, so I asked if he was angry with me. He slowly shook his head, no and said "Not really." Pointing to the ring I said, "Honey this ring is an investment. Later on if we become destitute we have this little gold mine to fall back on. As the years roll by, think about how it will increase in value. We will never be broke." We finished lunch with hardly a spoken word. For me to eat under such a strain was difficult to ingest my food. We drove home in silence and as he entered our circle driveway he cut the ignition. We sat in the car at home for a few minutes and as he reached for my hand, he turned the ring inward and said, "Wear this diamond inside the palm of your hand like this, (as he folded my fingers over the diamonds), do this every time you go out at night because someone will chop your finger off for that ring." I shook my head yes in the hopes he would say something endearing. He walked me to the front door and made no effort to come in. He said he had to get back to the office. When I asked when he was coming home; he only bowed his head and said I will call you. Not a word about the beauty of the ring or the expense, nor a sympathetic expression on his face for what I have been going through. He bowed his head and said good-bye. As I proceeded to open the front door I stood there and watched him drive away and he never looked back.

His office personal expressed concern and told me that something was amiss with my husband. I should pay more attention to his outside activities as they cautioned me. Originally it was his request that we say nothing about his leaving for a while so, no one, was aware he no longer lived at home.

My life became unbearable. For days, weeks, months, I appealed to Jack. If he did not call me I called him. Each meeting, every conversation set us further and further apart. My pushing and pleading only made him rebel even more. He professed all along that he was alone; no one else could possibly interest him that he simply needed time for himself. I tried to make him understand that such a statement was preposterous. He is alone so much of the time already. What kind of reasoning is that? The more distant he became, the harder I tried to make him want to come home, and the more he withdrew.

Attending church was devastating—memories would drag me down—but I prayed every day that he would appear at our front door. I couldn't bring myself to tell my parents or friends our ensuing problem. When they asked where Jack was or they invited us out, I always told them that he was away on business.

One of my dearest friends, Mary Primavera (God rest her soul), appealed to me one day after dinner. (Jack had accepted her invitation for dinner, but declined the last minute.) I attended alone in the hopes that Jack would be gracious enough to show up even if he was late. Mary said to me, "My dear, Joe and I love you and Jack so much and we are really worried about the two of you. Please kidnap your husband and take him out of the country for a couple of months. The both of you review your marriage vows and start living again for each other. Please, Rae, please do this now before it's too late. You have five beautiful sons, do this for them." I knew she was right. Jack had been gone for over a year already. How many more lies could I possibly tell? Where do I begin? God help me.

My mother, thinking that I'd be bored with being alone so much, introduced me to a company dealing in nutrition, skin care, and household items. The company, Shaklee Products, was based out of Hayward, California. I buried myself in work for this company. I thought back to the days when Jack first started in business, and I imitated all the things he did that made him successful. He taught me much more than he realized. I secured a distributorship, held meetings in our home at Rolling Hills, and I started traveling all over the country. My career kept me busy and helped me to stay sane. In six months I was awarded a new vehicle. I chose a beautiful white Ford LTD with maroon interior Never in my wildest dreams would I have ever believed I could succeed in such a venture. When the boys informed Dad about my success, it seemed to please him. There were times when I invited him to attend meetings with me, but he refused. From time to time he would check on where I was and what I was doing through the boys. I should have been checking on him.

Jack and I communicated between my business trips, and during one of our meetings at the house he asked me for a divorce. I went ballistic. My body started to shake uncontrollably and I screamed, *"No, absolutely not!"* He grabbed me and held me tight, bowed his head in my face and said, *"I'm so ashamed of myself."* I pleaded, "Please, honey, come home. I love you and I need you." I knew that he loved our sons and me, he did not want a divorce, and they're had to be an outside influence, but whom and why? But his blind determination to pursue his goal and his stubborn pride got the best of him.

I always told myself, "No matter what he dished out I could take and turn things around to both our satisfaction." He was going through difficult times in his life and I did not understand. I told myself that we are two grown individuals who understand each other; surely we can work this out between ourselves. Periodically he would assure me that he would be home soon. I believed him and I was certain he would return. But I was wrong. This is not to say that any of this was easy for him, because I know from the bottom of my heart that he suffered many times over as a result of his final decision.

He pressured me about the divorce for months. I relented only when he told me that, once I had signed the papers, he would realize just how much he really loved me and he would return home. (Since neither of us ever talked about our problems to anyone and no one knew he wasn't living at home, it would have been easy for him to just walk back in the front door and no one would have been the wiser.) He informed me that Dennis and I would be taken care of. I would receive regular subsistence (that is what he called it) and Dennis would be taken care of as long as he was in school. I thought to myself, this is insane. I said, "Honey please tell me, why should we go through all this malarkey if you mean what you are saying to me? I want to believe you, but you are talking about an additional tremendous expense. "Why, please tell me why?" But he was determined and said, "We are killing time for nothing. The sooner we get this started, the sooner I will be home." Foolishly I believed him.

He made plans to pick me up on the day I was to leave for New York. I was so upset and nervous when he arrived at the house; he said that we had to go to the Bank where we were to sign the papers. "Jack, I do not want to sign those papers." He would not listen. He grabbed my arm and we walked out the door. I prayed for God's forgiveness and, with a heavy heart and tears in my eyes, I tried to sign, but the bank personal touched my shoulder and said; "Perhaps the both of you should go home and think this over!" Jack immediately said, "No". I could not stop the tears and his hand shook so much, he had to stop, compose himself and then nervously he and I signed the documents together. I was so divested he had to help me out of the bank and into his car. The car would not start so he managed to call a taxi to take me to the airport. I wanted to die. It was so horrendous! He was upset too, but he went through it anyway.

Every day became increasingly difficult waiting for his return. It was a trick and I was unable to see the forest for the trees. Thinking back to those difficult days, I am not certain how I managed to stay in one piece. Receiving the final decree was one of the most painful experiences of my entire life. He made arrangements to leave me the house; he took a great deal of cash and all our shares of ARA stock. I was much too weak and too depressed to fight anymore.

The memories of Rolling Hills depressed me so much; finally I had no choice but to sell the property and relocate. Due to the slow economy it was a very bad time to sell but at this point I had already kept the house three long years. In order to keep my sanity I could stay no longer. Later I realized it would have been best if I had rented the property for a while.

I often wondered if I had listened to Mary in the first place, kidnap Jack and take him somewhere with just the two of us; no communication of any kind; would it have helped? Could we have saved our marriage? Could I have tricked him to going away with me for a few days? I really believe his pride was the determining factor. His mind was already made up.

After the divorce Jack married his private secretary. That union produced a daughter. I was not aware at that time that he had married again.

Each of the boys was deeply affected by this. It was so difficult for them, but they never left my side when I needed them. I could not, nor would I ever talk about our problem to anyone. So as not to overwhelm the boys with extra responsibility about me, I really worked hard at standing on my own two feet. Difficulties prevailed but some how I managed.

When Jack had his head on straight, he was the cream of the crop. He was tenacious, pragmatic, and nothing pretentious about him during our years together, but he always guarded his emotions. No matter how long I live and no matter what I do, I will never be more proud than I am this very minute for the life I spent with my husband and our five sons. My heart is so full of so much good that I cannot take anything away from what we had, or what we did for each other, or what we did together as a family. It was a beautiful and special marriage while it lasted. My only regret is that it ended much too soon.

Jack suffered a devastating stroke in1986. He underwent brain surgery to relieve the bleeding and pressure, but it did nothing for him. His illness robbed him of his speech and movement; he couldn't write, he knew what was going on around him but he was unable to communicate with anyone. Jack had always had an enormous appetite for life, and seeing him like this for so long was heartbreaking. He was cared for by different residential centers and that was very hard on him and very painful for me. Thanks to my brother-in-law McKinley Nutter who kept me informed as to his new residence allowing me the opportunity to visit him. On Valentine's Day I took him a bright red Teddy Bear and a small box of chocolates. He knew me and I could ascertain he was happy I was there. A smile from him to my questions was all I needed and I knew he understood.

I visited with him on four different occasions but on my last visit I found him in a wheel chair in his room. Seeing me brought a painful smile to his face. His elbow was on the arm of the chair and it seemed to me as if he was trying to greet me. I reached for his hands. My heart ached as I looked into his tired and painful eyes. I talked about things I knew he liked to hear. Remembering back to the days when I was so ill and could not talk, I reinitiated his exact words as he held me in his arms at that time. I said, *"I love you Mr. Nutter, and yes, I know you love me too."* He bowed his face breathing heavy as he squeezed my hands. I could feel the wetness of his tears and with tears in my eyes; I comforted him feeling within that he was at peace with himself knowing that I never stopped loving him. Shortly the nurse came. I bid him good-night with a promise I would return. He would squeeze my hands not wanting to let go so I helped the nurse get him down. I kissed his forehead, told him I would be back as I with drew my hands. I reached for my Kleenex and softly wiped his wet face. As I did this, his stare told he was trying to say something. I assured him that the boys loved him and would be in to see him soon. I wanted to stay until he went to sleep, but the nurse asked me to leave. As I drove home I found myself wishing there was something I could do to ease his suffering. Unfortunately it was the last time I saw him alive.

He became angry and difficult to get along with. Unable to bear up under the stress, he began to fight off anyone who tried to feed him. He lost fifty pounds, what little hair he had turned snow-white, and his face was a network of lines. This handsome, spirited man was scarcely recognizable. He wanted to go. His weakened condition caused him to contract pneumonia, and in 1991 he left for his heavenly abode.

Jack's body was cremated, and Patrick sprinkled part of his ashes over Jack's favorite golf course in Palos Verde When Grandpa Nutter died in 1994, Patrick took the remainder of his ashes to the funeral in Concordia, Kansas and laid them next to Grandpa in his coffin. Grandpa and Jack were very close, and we knew both of them would be happy being together.

Jack's passing was devastating to us in spite of our separation and final divorce. He was so special and we were so lucky to have him. In those early years he loved us as much as we loved him and he was always there when we needed him.

He made enormous personal family sacrifices over the years in order to succeed in his business but his contribution to society, to us as a husband, a father, and partner, will long endure. He was so supportive in raising our sons. He never lost his faith or patience with us and he gave us the happiest years of our lives. I am profoundly grateful to have been his wife and partner for those *twenty-six young years* together.

Our love for him has never faltered. This book is about our five sons, our lives together, and Jack's spirit shines through it all—through the things he held so dear over the years, the things he knew and felt important. Writing about our life together hasn't been easy, but the many beautiful and cherished memories have made the effort rich and worthwhile.

As he strummed his Ukulele before leaving on his business trips he would record a message to the boys and me. He always preached his usual to the boys regarding their behavior while he was gone, then he would say, "This is especially for you Mrs. Nutter," and he would sing a melody of songs but when he sang "When I Grow to Old to Dream," a song whose lyrics touched my heart but did not ease the loneliness I felt for him at the time he was gone. The tone in his voice was so sincere. His expression of love and devotion to me always made me feel special. I shall always be grateful for that alone. I cannot dwell on what should have been or what would have been; I simply had to embrace my life with pride and proceed along the beaten path with God's blessing.

This book brings a loving portrait of our lives together in our early years. Because of Jack's encouragement that I write memorable notes about the little boys early on; it is, with a great deal of pride that *I Proudly Dedicate* this book to him.

Jack Wilcox Nutter Sr.
September 28, 1923
Concordia, Kansas
Deceased—November 9, 1991
He was only sixty-eight years young

My Sons
Memoirs'

Jack Wilcox Nutter Jr.

Jack W. Nutter Jr.

DOB	February 25, 1947 Los Angeles, California
1960	Graduated St. Johns Jr School Fresno, California
1964	Graduated Fermin Lasuen High School San Pedro, California
1964 to 1966	Attended Harbor College (September) San Pedro, California
1966	(December) U.S.N. Reserves
1967 to 1968	Electronics "A" School (April 67 to 68) Treasure Island
1968	Electronics "C" School (April 68 to July 68) Mare Island
1968 to 1970	Northwest Cape, Exmouth, Australia (Aug. 68 to Feb 70)
1970 to 1971	Navcmsta Asmara, Ethipopia (Feb. 70 to Aug. 71) (Navcomsta Harold E. Holt)
1971 to 1972	U.S.S. Forrestal (CVA-59) (Oct. 71–Dec. 72)
1972	Anniversary Discharge (December 12, 1972)

Married has two Sons, One Daughter
Resides in Las Vegas, Nevada

Commanding
Officer
CDR Douglas F.
Smiley,
USNAVCOMSTA
Asmara, present
and
Congratulates
ETN 2
Jack W. Nutter
with
*Good Conduct
Medal*
In ceremonies
held in
The Tract "F"
Theater on
7 April 1971

29 January 1970

From: Commanding Officer
To: ETN2 Jack Wilcox NUTTER Jr., USN, B82 66 71

Subj: Letter of Commendation

1. During your tour at U.S. Naval Communication Station, Harold
E. Holt, you consistently distinguished yourself in numerous
ways. Your extensive knowledge of transmitter maintenance and
your desire to learn made you the most valuable High Frequency
Transmitter maintenance technician at the site. You employed
your knowledge in training new technicians and in solving
equipment problems which arose during both duty and liberty
hours. Your exceptional ability in establishing quality control procedures as well as diagnosing equipment troubles
assisted the command in establishing DCA standards. Additionally, you devoted many extra hours performing maintenance
on crypto equipment at the Communication Center, as there were
no other qualified personnel to perform these tasks.

2. While at this command you were an active member of the
Welfare and Recreation Committee. As a committee member, you
dedicated yourself to improving recreational facilities, and
encouraged participation in the Intramural sports program, by
organizing division flag football and bowling teams, and by com-
peting in softball and basketball activities. You also actively
served in the preparation of the children's Christmas party by
helping in purchasing and wrapping gifts.

3. Although single and residing on the station, you actively
participated in community activities, promoting fellowship and
understanding between Australians and Americans. The untiring
efforts you made in local fund raising campaigns for Spastic
Children's Society of Australia and Merrilinga Kindergarten
Association were commendable. You also assisted in the com-
pletion and landscaping of the kindergarten building and were
active in conducting a Halloween parade in the townsite for
Australian and American children.

4. It is with great pleasure that I commend you for your highly
professional performance of duty, and the leadership displayed
in both military duties and community relations. You have been
a valuable asset to this station, and your services will be
sorely missed.

Subj: Letter of Commendation

5. A copy of this letter will be made a part of your service
record.

H. H. FREELAND

Patrick James Nutter

Patrick James Nutter

DOB March 12, 1948
1963 Graduated Mary Mount Junior High
       Palos Verdes Estates, California
1966 Graduated Rolling Hills, High School
       Rolling Hills, California
1967 Entered Harbor College
       San Pedro, California
1967 Enlisted United States Navy (September 1967)
1967 Boot Camp San Diego, California
1969 Signalman School (Four Weeks)
1969 Signalman Quarter Master Third Class
1969 USS Lucid (Mso-458) (August 1969
       Embarked for Pearl Harbor, Hawaii
          Yokuska Japan, On to Korea, Taiwan
          Singapoe, Bangkok Thailand, Vietnam
          Subie Bay Philippines, Guam Kwajalein
          In the Marshall Island
1970 Return to Pearl Harbor and on to Long Beach, Ca.
1970 USS Lucid was decommissioned in December
1971 Honorable Discharge (March 1971)

Married has two sons, one daughter
Resides in Lomita, California

Patrick Aboard U. S. S. Lucid

COMMANDING OFFICER
U.S.S. LUCID (MSO-458)
FLEET POST OFFICE
SAN FRANCISCO. 96601

16 June 1969

Dear Mr. & Mrs. Nutter,

I wish to take this opportunity to
congratulate you on your son's recent
advancement to Signalman Third Class.

The United States Navy is responsible
for maintaining control of the sea and is
a ready force on watch at home and overseas,
capable of strong action to preserve the
peace or of instant offensive action to
win in war. Tradition, valor and victory
are the Navy's heritage from the past. Ded-
ication, discipline and vigilance are the
watchwords of the present and future.

Your son's advancement carries with it
greater responsibilities and thereby makes
him a more integral part of the USS LUCID,
the Navy and the overall defense effort of
the United States of America. Never have
our opportunities and our responsibilities
been greater.

Commanding

244

Terrill Mark Nutter

Terrill Mark Nutter

DOB	May 3, 1949
1964	Graduated Marymont Grade School
	Palos Verdes Peninsula
1967	Graduated Rolling Hills High School
	Rolling Hills Estates, California
1967–1969	Harbor College, San Pedro, California
1970	Enlisted United States Army (February 1970)
1970	Fort Ord BCT Brigade (Basic Combat Training)
	AIT School (Advanced Infantry Training)
	Fort Benning Georgia NCO School
	(Non-Commissioned Officer)
1971	Shipped to Vietnam (February 1971)
	173 Airbone Brigade
1971	Returns to Fort Benning Georgia
1971	Stateside with Honorable Discharge
	From Active Service (November 1971)

Married has four sons, three daughters
Resides North of Brisbane, Australia

17 April 1970

Mr. and Mrs. Jack W. Nutter
6 Caestefield Road
Rolling Hills, California 90274

Dear Mr. and Mrs. Nutter:

Your son, Private Terrill M. Nutter, Company C, 4th Battalion, Third BCT Brigade, Fort Ord, California, has been selected as a Distinguished Trainee in his company. The selection was made by the officers and non-commissioned officers of his company and was based on his soldierly attributes, personal conduct, and his ability to assimilate the training presented.

As his parents, you may feel justifiable pride in your son's military accomplishments. His excellent spirit of cooperation, combined with an obvious desire to excel, are the principal personal characteristics which produced the outstanding results that he achieved. These personal attributes characterize not only good soldiers, but also good citizens. I am proud to have been your son's commander.

Sincerely yours,

PAUL E. NOTTAGE
Colonel, Infantry
Commanding

Terry March 12, 1970

Michael Gregory Nutter

Michael Gregory Nutter
Attorney at Law
Long Beach, California

DOB	May 10, 1950
	Graduated Dapplegrey Jr. High School
	Palos Verdes, California
1968–1970	Entered Harbor College, San Pedro, California
1970–1072	California State University of Dominguez Hills
	BA in Psychology
1973–1976	Pepperdine University, JD
1977	State Bar of California
1978–1979	Law Office of Roberts and Thompson
1979–1980	Law Office of Roberts, Thomas and Nutter Partner
1982	Orange County Harbor Municipal Court
	Judge Pro Tem
1982–1983.1	Fountain Valley Jaycee
1984–1985	California Jaycees Lt. Dist. Gov.
	Honors:
	Rotary Club, Rotarian of the Year
1983–1986	Fountain Valley Jaycees, Dir. Of the Qtr
1983	Hustler Award
1984	California Jaycees, Success Express Award
1985	Yes We Can Award
1986	Silver Nugget Award

Has three sons, one daughter
Resides in Long Beach, California

Dennis Paul Nutter

Dennis Paul Nutter DDS

THE AMERICAN BOARD OF
PEDIATRIC DENTISTRY
INCORPORATED 1940

ORGANIZED THROUGH THE COOPERATION OF THE AMERICAN SOCIETY OF DENTISTRY FOR CHILDREN
AND THE AMERICAN DENTAL ASSOCIATION
SPONSORED SINCE 1964 BY THE AMERICAN ACADEMY OF PEDIATRIC DENTISTRY
Hereby Certifies That

DENNIS PAUL NUTTER
DECEMBER 15, 1995

HAS MET ALL REQUIREMENTS OF THIS BOARD AND IS HEREBY CERTIFIED AS A DIPLOMATE IN THE SPECIALTY OF

PEDIATRIC DENTISTRY

DOB	October 23, 1952
1966	Graduated Dapplegrey Jr. High School\ Palos Verdes, California
1970	First Graduating Class of Miraleste High School Miraleste California
1975	University of Southern California (January) Bachelors of Science Biology
1975	Post Graduate Class of New York University "The Psychology of Aesthetics."
1975	Delivery Driver for Stainless Steel Fabrication Company in factory sums of Brooklyn N. Y.
1975	Witnessed a robbery/murder in Brooklyn
1975	Entered USC School of Dentistry (August)
1979	Doctor of Dental Surgery, USC
1979	Testified in murder trial in New York City (May) Identified the murderer, told my story and he was sent Away for 25 years. This bad guy was captured near the USC School of Dentistry just before my State Boards Ironically, when I testified, the murdered man's son was In his second year of Dental School of NYU
1979–1980	Private practice in Long Beach, California
1980–1982	Private Practice in San Jose and Santa Clara, California
1984	Completed two years Hospital Residency in Pediatric Dentistry, USC, Rancho Los Amigos Hospital, Downey, Ca. California's Hospital L A. California
1984	Los Angeles: Passed written exam section of Pediatric Dental Boards
1989	Boston: Passed Oral Exam section of Pediatric Dental Boards
1995	San Francisco: Passed Comprehensive Simulation Exam section of Pediatric Dental Boards

December 18, 1999—Passed all section of the Clinical Site visit Componet of the Pediatric Dental Boards. Given Diplomate Board Certified status on that date. Only 30% of Pediatric Dentist are Board Certified due to the ardunos nature of these boards.

We are the only Board Certified Pediatric Dentist in Napa and Salano Counties

Married has one son
Resides in Vacaville, California

Grandchildren's Birthdays

1. Rodney Jack Nutter   09/04/75
2. Tracy Lynn Nutter   10/12/76
3. Scott Patrick Nutter   04/21/78
4. Laura Ilene Nutter   09/05/80
5. Christopher James Nutter   07/25/81
6. Timothy Mark Nutter   11/07/82
7. Gregory James Nutter   08/10/84
8. Miriam Ruth Nutter   09/08/84
9. Eric Michael Nutter   10/30/85
10. Elizabeth Rachel Nutter   06/13/86
11. Aaron Trevor Nutter   02/24/87
12. Travis Branning Nutter   09/15/87
13. Marc Jgofrey Nutter   03/06/88
14. Andrew James Nutter   09/20/88
15. Sarah Rebekah Nutter   04/08/89
16. Renee Michael Nutter   05/10/90
17. Johathan Paul Nutter   10/22/91
18. Joel Andrew Nutter   12/16/93

Great Grand Children

1. Jackson Thor Nutter (San Diego California)   06/15/2004
       Dad & Mom—Rodney J and Sadie Nutter

2. Raden Waric Terry (Layetteville, No. Carolina) 12/27/2004
       Mom & Dad Tracy and Ian Terry

3. Levi Mark McKinlay (Queensland, Australia)   05/31/2006
       Mom & Dad—Miriam and David McKinlay

4. Tallulah Jane Nutter (Bosi Idaho)   10/10/2006
       Dad & Mom—Rodney J. and Sadie Nutter

5. Laden Reese Nutter (Costa Mesa, California)   12/15/2006
       Mom—Nicole D Kempt & Dad—Gregory James Nutter

6. River Elise Terry (Ewa Beach, Hawaii)   02/05/2007
       Mom & Dad—Tracy and Ian Terry